Insights from the Spirit

The early Christian ministries of

Jean Morris nee Deans:

Lost notes and Messages

Helen Brown

Reading Stones Publishing

Copyright © Helen Brown 2024

ISBN   Softcover   978-1-923021-14-3
        eBook   978-1-923021-15-0

All rights reserved. No part of this book may be reproduced or transmitted in any form or by any means, electronic, or mechanical, including photocopying, recording or by any information storage and retrieval system without the permission in writing by the copyright owner.

Unless otherwise stated Scriptures quoted here are from the King James Version (Authorised version). First published in 1611. Quoted from the KJV Classic Reference Bible, copyright 1983 by the Zondervan Corporation.

Published by: Reading Stones Publishing
Helen Brown & Wendy Wood
Woodwendy1982.wixsite.com/readingstones

Cover Design By: Craft-to-Cover by Wendiilou
                    Wendy Wood

For more copies contact the author at:

Glenburnie Homestead
212 Glenburnie Road
ROB ROY NSW 2360
Mobile: 0422 577 663
Email: readingstonespublishing@gmail.com

This book is dedicated to the memory of my mother, Jean Olwyn Morris who was not only a faithful servant of God, her saviour, but also my greatest mentor and best friend.

Index

Broadcast 2	10
Broadcast 2PK – Christmas	14
Broadcast 2 PK – Parks Home League	17
Broadcast 2PK – 31 May 1962	20
Broadcast 2PK 3	22
Broadcast 2PK 4 – New Year	24
Broadcast 2PK 6	26
Broadcast 2PK 7	29
Broadcast 2PK 8	32
Broadcast 2PK 10	34
Broadcast 2PK 22 – World Day of Prayer	37
Broadcast Ayr Holiness 2PK	40
Broadcast 2PK 9 – 15 December 1960	42
Broadcast 2MG 1	46
Broadcast 2MG 2	49
Broadcast 2MG 3	51
Broadcast 2MG4 – Women's Forum	54
1961 Christmas Breakup	57
A refuge	59

Acts 3:1-16	61
Be Strong in the Lord	66
Be Afternoon	71
Behold the Lamb of God	73
Being an Example	76
Being Humble	79
Books and Gadgets	80
Children of Israel	81
Christmas in the Home No 3	84
Christmas in the Home No 5	87
Cleaning the Temple	89
Crusade Home League Dubbo	91
Cups	96
Dolls	99
Five Senses	101
God is Love	105
Good Work	108
Harvest Thanksgiving 18 March 1951	111
Holiness	114
How Committed are You	117

Lord, I Believe	120
Love our Enemies	123
Men seek Better Methods	125
Mother's Day	128
Our Bodies – God's Temple	130
Our Modern Civilization	133
Prophecy Against the House of Eli	137
Right or Wrong	139
The story of Joseph	141
My friend – Mrs Griffey	143

Author notes

This book is compiled out of some of the notes left by my mother. There are plenty of materials that have not been used in this book, hence the discrepancy in some of the numbering, but may be used in future publications. My mother served God faithfully through her ministry with The Salvation Army, and in her home, up until her death in 2014. This book is being published in her memory and to celebrate her life, ten years after her passing.

She entered The Salvation Army Training College, in Sydney as Cadet Jean Olwyn Deans in 1950 and served as:

1951 Probationary Lieutenant to Ayr (assisting 1st Lt Jean Bird - still alive)

1952 Second Lieutenant to Mt Morgan (assisting) then to Stanthorpe (assisting Heather Gardner)

1953 Second Lieutenant to Blackbutt (assisting Iris Armstrong)

1954 Second Lieutenant to Paddington (NSW)

1954 Second Lieutenant to Botany

1955 promoted to First Lieutenant to Nambour as an assistant and then briefly to Laidley

Her marriage on January 7, 1956, to Second Lieutenant Norman Morris (Riverview Qld), saw her go from First Lieutenant to Second Lieutenant the same rank as her husband. Together they served as Salvation Army Officers at Mt Isa, Canowindra, Parks, Mudgee, and Toowong. After resigning as Officers, they continued to serve the Lord at Inverell, Bingara, Warialda, and finally Gympie.

These notes are a collection of her radio broadcasts, sermons, small group gatherings, Bible studies, and guest appearances. These notes reflect the different era and language that was used at the time. Some notes were incomplete or damaged and so were partly lost, therefore, I have edited or interpreted them in line with my weekly telephone conversations held over the many years that we lived miles apart. I am thankful for all of assistance and encouragement from family members and friends.

Despite the language and the different times, the messages are still the same, the Grace of God is eternal, the love of God wants all of us to return to a relationship with Him through the saving blood of Jesus who died for all our sins on the cross.

My prayer is that God's Holy Spirit, will continue to do an amazing work through what He started through her all those years ago.

Helen Brown

Broadcast 2

I would like to read two well-known poems today, but can we stop and make sure that the familiarity of the words does not rob us of the challenge of the questions and truths.

If Jesus Came To Your House
by Lois Blanchard Eades (1956)

If Jesus came to your house to spend a day or two -
If He came unexpectedly, I wonder what you'd do.
Oh, I know you'd give your nicest room to such an honored Guest,
And all the food you'd serve to Him would be the very best,
And you would keep assuring Him you're glad to have him there -
That serving Him in your own home is joy beyond compare.

But when you saw Him coming, would you meet Him at the door
With arms outstretched in welcome to your heavenly visitor?
Or would you have to change your clothes before you let

Him in?
Or hide some magazines and put the Bible where they'd been?
Would you turn off the radio and hope He hadn't heard?
And wish you hadn't uttered that last, loud, hasty word?

Would you hide your worldly music and put some hymn books out?
Could you let Jesus walk right in, or would you rush about?
And I wonder - if the Savior spent a day or two with you,
Would you go right on doing the things you always do?
Would you go right on saying the things you always say?
Would life for you continue as it does from day to day?

Would your family conversation keep up its usual pace?
And would your find it hard each meal to say a table grace?
Would you sing the songs you always sing, and read the books your read,
And let Him know the things on which your mind and spirit feed?
Would you take Jesus with you everywhere you'd planned to go?
Or would you, maybe, change your plans for just a day or so?

Would you be glad to have Him meet your very closest friends?

Or would you hope they'd stay away until His visit ends?
Would you be glad to have Him stay forever on and on?
Or would you sigh with great relief when He at last was gone?
It might be interesting to know the things that you would do
If Jesus Christ in person came to spend some time with you.

What a challenge to us all – what will you do with Jesus, neutral you cannot be. Someday your heart will be asking, "What will He do with me?"[1]

The second poem gives one writer's response to this all-important question.

I stood alone at the bar of God.

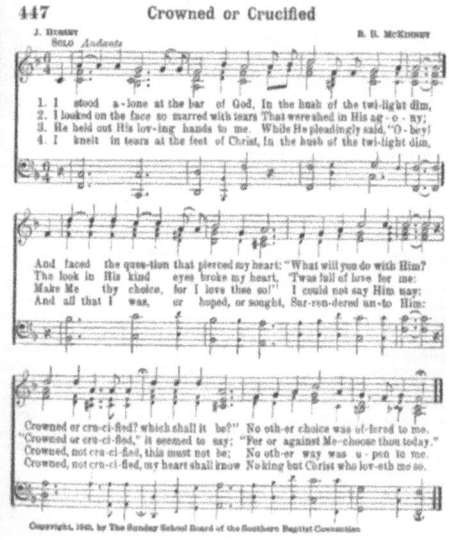

I must do something with Jesus – you must do something with Jesus. What are we doing with Him? Are we shutting him out of our business, pleasure, our homes, our personal lives? Many of us would not want him to come for even a few days' visit. If this is the case, He is crucified afresh by us, which is saying in plain language we will not have this man to rule over us. It cannot end here because, like the hymn written by Isacc Watts in 1719 says, "for Jesus, shall reign where are the sun doth it successive journey run."

He is King of all, and we reject Him at our own peril for if we deny Him, he will deny us.

Can you say with the Old-fashioned revival Hour quartette, "Blessed assurance Jesus is mine."[2] "Crowned King and Lord of my life"[3]. If you cannot, then will you make Christ King while these lovely words are being sung.

Let's us Pray: Some of our listeners have welcomed you into their heart, home, and all of life is under your divine direction. Bless those today we pray. Some are thinking of what it will mean, help them now to see what the consequences will be to reject you. Lord, give them the grace to say all that I am, and all have shall be yours.

---

[1] Albert B. Simpson 1905
[2] Hymn -David Thomas Clydesdale
[3] Jennie Evelyn Hussey 1874-1958

Broadcast 2Pk

Christmas – Home League[1] Parks

"Glory to God in the Highest, Peace on earth, goodwill to men."[2] How wonderful it would have been to hear the angels' song, but when we look closely at the happenings of that time, we are led to ask.

Would it seem to those connected to this event that glory was being brought to God and peace among men? Would Mary and Joseph have a tinge of disappointment that a cattle shed was all they could find for such a wonderful event? They were told He was to be the Son of the Highest. Was it glorifying to God to bring His son into the world without proper sterilisation, among the smell of cattle, with the risk of germs, was it hospital standard for men working among sheep to gather around a newborn baby.

Was it glorifying God for the wise men to have to go back secretly to their own country? Why couldn't they tell the king and have all Jerusalem learn the wonderful news? Was it glorifying God when Joseph had to gather his few belongings and escape quietly at night with Jesus, who was only a very small boy, and rush off to a new country, strange people, insecurity, finding work, and all that is entailed in a move.

Did the angels really mean peace on earth when they sang?

Was it peace to the country when Herod demanded the death of every boy up to two years of age. Women crying because solders marched in and took from their arms their baby boys. When fathers tried in vain to protect and even rescue their sons. Was it peace for the soldiers, some themselves fathers, who were forced to destroy these screaming innocent little ones.

Fleeing for ones' life to another country is not our idea of peace nor would it have been theirs.

Where then does this lovely song that we enjoy so much now come, in those days. Why was there so much turmoil and unrest. It was goodness and purity coming face to face with wickedness and sin and sin forever will cause turmoil in its conflict with right. There is no peace saith my God to the wicked.[3]

There is only peace when the evil has been conquered and the prince of peace reigns in full control.

Did these happenings really bring glory to God as the Angels sang. If Christ was born in a palace, you and I and others wouldn't know what to do in those surroundings. We all can feel at ease in these lowliest of circumstances. There was nothing to detract from the glory of God's lovely gift. No one felt out of place, no one was more interested in the beauty of the surroundings than the beauty of the baby.

Sin is seen in all its horror and cruelty which shows such a gleaming contrast to God's amazing love and giving of himself. When God gives His best, Satan does his worst.

Evil will always endeavour to destroy the right, but because of God's great gift of His son, and Christ's great sacrifice of himself, there is victory for those who believe in Him, then there is peace in the heart, goodwill to others, and glory to God.

---

[1] **Author's Note,** The Salvation Army's Home League was created by Florence Booth, daughter-in-law of the Army's founder, for practical and religious instruction for women. The first Home League meeting was held in London in 1907. By an order from territorial headquarters in Melbourne, the league was inaugurated throughout Australasia in March 1911. In about 1940, the purposes of the Home League were succinctly summarised as worship, education, fellowship, and service.
[2] Luke 2:14
[3] Isaiah 48:22

Broadcast 2PK

Parkes Home League

This month I read two interesting articles in the Readers Digest - The confessions of a colour-blind male and an article about a famous Japanese artist. I found these interesting because it helped me on a line of thought. I want to share that thought with you today.

Apparently, there are a great many more people than we realize who do not really see colours as they are, for example they see red as a 'kind of light black'. The cry of this Japanese artist was that after years of study and hard work, he had not yet learned to draw things as they really are.

This ability to see things as they really are could well occupy our thinking for a while.

After running around in circles for a while my small son sits down and quite startled, exclaims "the house is going round". To him it is the house out of gear not him. How often have you seen the boards on a boat deck, literally moving, after you have looked for a while at the moving water. Our eyes do deceive us whether we like to admit it or not.

Have you been for an eye test and discovered that one eye has seen one thing, and the other has seen that same thing in a different place? Physically does not it depend on the balance and the working together of our entire system as to how we see things.

This leads me to the further thought of spiritual perception. Does not this too depend on spiritual balance if I am to see spiritual realities as they really are.

Have not things become out of proportion, distorted when we have been over wrought or emotionally upset? Do not insignificant things become great issues when we are worried and het up? Do we then see things as they really are?

If Spiritual things are unreal, blurred, or distorted, could it not be that we are unbalanced?

Down through the ages, men have looked at Christ and so many have not seen Him as He really is. He tested them out once when He was on earth. "Who do men say that I am?"[1]

How did they see Him? Some saw in Him as a prophet, some saw Elijah come back, some John the Baptist. Peter saw Him as the Christ the Son of the living God. How do you see Him? As a good man, as a great teacher, as a figure in history, as someone remote and unreal. Is this what He really is? How can you be sure you are seeing Him a right?

I cannot argue you into clear a perception of Christ. I cannot even prove to you that He is real. I can only say the same as some writers of Scripture, "we speak to that we do know and testify to that we have seen"[2] and so I say today, I would like you to meet Him for yourself because once you have met Him, He will be real. He will be great; He will be more than life itself. Where can you meet Him? "You Shall seek me and find me when you shalt seek for me with all your heart".[3]

---

[1] Matthew 16:13-19
[2] John 3:11
[3] Jeremiah 29:13

Broadcast 2PK

31 May 1962

What is your attitude towards the ordinary things of life? I like the attitude of Jesus towards ordinary things. He took so many common everyday things and taught valuable and important lessons by them. Take the everyday thing that we all use so much, a gate. Well, to you perhaps it might mean very little, a gate's a gate and that's that. It was to me too until a few years ago when God taught me an important lesson through a gate, but first of all, let's think of it as a means of entry. The shape and design doesn't mean much, it either keeps people and animals out or lets them in. If it's locked, you stay out or in, unless you have the key. Jesus told us there are two gates in life. One of which we must enter, one is a big wide gate opening onto a very wide road, the other is a small narrow gate opening onto a narrow path. At first glance, the wide one is the most inviting, it's the easiest, it's the most popular, it's the most attractive, but there's one serious thing wrong with this gate. It's the gateway to hell and it's entered in this life not the next. So many have gone through that gate because it's easy and haven't stopped to think where it's leading. The other is hard to enter, but Jesus said to strive to enter this gate. It is worth the greatest effort we can make, for it leads to eternal life with God in Heaven. Once a person comes through the gate of our homes they are on our properly and we have the right to invite them to stay or ask them to leave. So, to each life comes Christ and we have the opportunity to invite Him to stay or ask Him to leave. If He leaves because He's not invited, then Satan can do his worst in our souls.

Jean and Gate at Canowindra.[1]

At Canowindra we had a gate that needed to be lifted slightly in order to stop it dragging through the dirt while it was being opened. Our daughter was two at the time and wanted to help me one morning to open it so my husband could leave for work. I lifted, and while I was doing that, she had no problem pushing the gate, she thought she was able to do this all by herself, so she told me to go away and let her continue on her own. But as soon as I let go, the gate dropped down into the dirt and pushing became too hard for her small body. The lesson for me was that while we allow God to help us, things can go much smoother but as soon as we try to do things on our own, then we find that we struggle to accomplish many of the things we are called to do.

---

[1] Authors Note, as told to me by my mother.

Broadcast 2PK 3

Luke 10:38

Many of us today complain about being over busy. Duties are always waiting to be done and we are laden with cares and worries from morning to night. The 24 hours are never long enough for all we must do. But very often our hurry is unnecessary there being much movement and very little progress. Our fears and anxieties keep us very busy. It is not the task that our trade or position in life places upon us, it is the work and worry which, utterly unnecessary, we impose upon ourselves. Some expected trouble takes hold of our minds, and we are haunted at every turn by it. Some real or fancied slight irritates, and we find no rest. We become embittered.

A cure for this unrest is found in the attitude of Mary. She sat at the feet of Christ, intent only on hearing His word. We need a mind at leisure from itself. The soul occupied by God is the only free soul. The mind filled with God is the only one that has leisure to do its best in the world. Many a person who has the credit of being worn out with work, is really worn out with worry, and worry usually means self. If we desire to accomplish more in this world, we must obtain more leisure, that is leisure from ourselves, the self that steals our time, and wears out our powers. When we surrender this self-life, He gives us abundant life. Life that enables us to take up unattempted tasks and new burdens and carry them easily. Find leisure to be alone with God and He will give you leisure from yourself.

This larger life can be lived here. There are men whom no burdens or even misfortunes can daunt them because their minds and hearts are filled with God. We think of Stephen, the martyr, who, when being stoned to death, did not feel the stones because he looked up and saw God.

Let us take the words of Jesus, "Come unto me, all ye that labour and are heavy laden and I will give you rest.[1] Rest is not a hallowed feeling that comes over us in church or service, but the repose of a heart set deep in God. It is the word of a man who can say with Browning, 'God's in His heaven, all's well with the world.'

"Let not self, hold any part; all we lay before thee.
Be thou conqueror of each heart.
We as one, implore thee."[2]

---

[1] Matthew 11:28
[2] From We the people of Thy Host, Emma Booth-Tucker

Broadcast 2PK 4

New Year

Have you made New Year Resolutions, did you decide; – 'I want to be just like Jesus – Kind and Good'?

We are not in the realm of doing but being. We are so taken up with doing that we forget that being is more important. "But of him are ye in Christ Jesus, who of God is made unto us wisdom, and righteousness, and sanctification, and redemption:"[1] Already have you done the same things as you did last year despite any resolutions? Why, we ask, is it that the old habits keep coming back?

Take the word HABIT.

If we remove a bit such as the 'H' we are left with "A bit." If remove a bit more, for instance the 'A', we are still left with "bit" and even if we take the "b" out, we are still left with "it."

The trouble lies in trying to do the breaking of habits by ourselves. Christ is not taken as our pattern. He is not taken as our power.

Do we really want to be good and kind like Jesus or are we afraid people will think we are soft, weak, or a goody, goody two shoes? How kind are we to those around us? Do we ever get outside of ourselves just enough to think up ways of being kind? Kind to dad, mum, husband, wife, children, relatives, neighbours, business associates, church friends, casual acquaintances, bakers, milkmen, and so many we touch all the time. They all are gladdened by kindness and inspired by goodness? Jesus is the answer to the problem of self that we all face. Jesus spoke of denying self, taking up the cross and following Him.[2] It is a hard, long road and it is not for the weak, or spineless but Christ will come Himself to us with the power, with His Spirit, if we receive Him, we will become new creatures in Christ Jesus.

---

[1] 1 Cor 1:30
[2] Matthew 16:24

Broadcast 2PK 6

Character, not circumstances, determines usefulness in God's Service. If this is so, God uses me, but do not circumstances have a big influence on how I can be used by God?

How often we concentrate on our circumstances and chafe (become annoyed) because we feel they are against us. So often we want them changed and say 'if I lived in a better neighbourhood, if I had better conditions at work. If there was a higher standard kept by the people with whom I work, it would be much easier to be good'. We say our circumstances limit us and we cannot do what we want to do for God and others. Could we but remember that character determines what we can do for God.

Even a person isolated from others can do such a tremendous amount for God if he or she is a Godly, praying person, for more is done by prayer than we can ever imagine. A letter written to someone can be such a blessing if it is written from a sincere loving heart. Even the ordinary life of every day can be an acceptable offering to God if our hearts are in tune with Him. We might have great opportunities and yet we can be absolutely useless in God's sight because our characters are not equal to the task. It is a case of getting past our circumstances and down deeper to our real selves.

The source of Character – A person of Character is a person of quality. Nothing can claim quality if its only good on the outside. People in Christ's day were like this, and Jesus said they were like whited sepulchres,[1] and did not call them men of character. "As he thinketh in his heart so is he."[2] So, character is what we are, and this marks the degree to which God uses us. As in most things we tend to think only on the earthly, the visible, the outside. We think so much about our circumstances probably because we often cannot do anything about changing them, so little thought is given to how they have a bearing on the extent of my usefulness? When God wants to use a person, he does not look for someone in good and desirable circumstances, but for someone after His own heart, someone of character, and uses them often in spite of their circumstances. The eyes of the Lord run to and fro throughout the whole earth to show himself strong on the behalf of them whose hearts are perfect toward him.[3] True, our circumstances do limit us, but they do not limit God and if we are doing things for God in our own way, we have reason to feel hampered by circumstances, but difficult situations only give God a greater opportunity to display His power. We find ourselves in undesirable circumstances sometimes because of our own folly. Then our usefulness still depends on getting our hearts right, receiving courage to change what we can and allowing God to work His will in spite of the rest.

Character is something that can only be changed by ourselves with God, by this I mean, we must decide, at some point, whether we will allow God to make us good quality right through.

---

[1] Matthew 23:27
[2] Proverbs 23:7
[3] 2 Chronicles 16:9

Broadcast 2Pk 7

Philippians 4:22

Here Paul addresses the Saints in Caesar's household which speaks to us of their goodness under trying conditions. Many complain that it is hard for them to be good because they live or work under difficult circumstances. Some have quarrelsome neighbours, a nagging wife, a drunken husband, and 101 reasons why they cannot be good. Of course, goodness is seen much more clearly under such conditions. We think of Abigail in Old Testament days.[1] She had a wealthy husband. It could have been easy, but it was not – with 3,000 sheep, 1,000 goats, and property extended over two or three miles which was quite a considerable holding in that time. Shearing sheds at Carmel while he lived at Maon. He was churlish, wicked. So low that people could not speak to him. David and his 600 men had helped Nabal in protecting his sheep. They were hungry at times, yet not once did one of them steal a sheep. David felt in view of all this and Nabal's prosperity quite justified in asking a gift of provisions for his men. Nabal not only refused but was very rude. David received this refusal in a spirit of revenge, prepared for war and intended to wipe him off the map. A servant told Abigail who, beautiful as she was, was also wise and kind. She sent 200 loaves of bread, 2 bottles wine, 5 dressed sheep, 5 measures of dried corn, 100 clusters of raisins, 200 cakes of figs. She went to David herself, asked forgiveness for the wrong and prevented David from doing something which he would have most certainly regretted. Vengeance belongs to God. David was grateful and assured Abigail of peace. When she arrived home, a party was in progress, Nabal was drunk, so she quietly waited till the morning. Because of his loose living, his health had suffered and when she told him of the very close escape from death, because of her intervention, the shock brought on a heart attack, and he was unconscious for 10 days and died. David, realizing the qualities of this good woman under such circumstances, asked for her to become his wife. She felt unworthy to be the wife of such a man as David but said she would be happy to be the servant to wash the feet of his servants. She was, however, made his wife and was abundantly rewarded for her faithfulness and consistent goodness under trying conditions. God sees and rejoices over such faithfulness, and will most certainly reward those who endure, drawing from Him the grace and strength to stand firm for the right and remain faithful through all.

Prayer: O God you know all the long and unhappy record of human struggle and misery and the evil which is constantly at war with all goodness. We thank thee that we know right must win because thou art God, Thou art good. Teach us to draw from thy grace that we might show thy power and love under all circumstances.

---

[1] 1 Samuel 25

Broadcast 2PK 8

We all enjoy looking at jewels. What woman's heart is not gladdened by the sight of a lovely diamond ring, or a jewel set in a brooch. If we were in the city, we could wander around the museum and see thousands of precious stones and minerals. As we look at these, we marvel that there are so many colours, markings, shapes, and varieties. It is impossible to say which is the best for they are all wonderful and what would appeal to me, for some reason, would not mean as much to you perhaps as some other. Most of these come from the ground, but one comes from the sea. You know, of course, that is the pearl. One of the stories I liked best in the geography lessons was the story of the western coast of Australia and the pearl diving. Extremely interesting to learn how the pearl is formed. A little speck of sand or foreign matter gets into the shell and irritates the oyster and over a long period, this irritation brings into being the lovely pearl. The shah of Persia gave £180,000 for a pearl and it is also said that Cleopatra gave £80,000 for one. The finest pearl the world has ever seen was found off the West Australian coast and the largest, called the Beresford-Hope Pearl, weighed 1,800 grams - over six times as much as the oyster that produced it.

Some time ago I was given a very lovely book written by Charys E Biglice called a Necklace of Perfect Joy. In this book she sets out to tell some of the experiences that came to her as a missionary in the dark land of Africa. This is what she says when a little pleasure has flashed for a moment against the dark, I have made that jewel mine. I have hundreds of them, I call it my necklace of Perfect Joy. When the world goes wrong I have only to close my eyes and remember all the links in my chain set with gems, some large and some small, but all beautiful with the beauty that never fades. My necklace of Perfect Joy will bring me happiness to the end, when I shall put it on, to be never more unclasped. In this lovely necklace of Perfect Joy, she has included, among others, a cluster of rubies for love, the emerald of hope, moonstone for merriment, pure jade for purity, and some lovely pearls of peace. (Read Pearls of Peace from Necklace of Perfect Joy.)

Broadcast 2PK 10

We greet our friends far and near at the closing of another day. Has it been a good day? Have you known peace today? Have you felt the Saviour near? Have you prayed today? And then we perhaps should ask ourselves, how have we prayed? Benjamin Ambler in his poem: "How do we pray" reveals a solemn truth.

How do we Pray

I wonder what are the payers I pray
As seen from the other side,
I am still petitioning day by day,
For something that is denied.

Some gift I am certain would make life sweet,
And help me to grow in grace,
Would nerve my heart, and would speed my feet
For running the Christian race.

I would give some service that is not asked
I would say what my work should be,
I would not mind how severely tasked
Did the choice but remain with me.

So, I miss the power that can surely save,
When I pray - As I have begun
So often, give me the thing I crave
So seldom, Thy will be done.

"Many believed on Him, they did not confess him. They loved the praise of men more than the praise of God."[1] Inwardly they believed in Christ, outwardly they denied him. They were afraid of being excommunicated from the Synagogue which was the centre of Jewish life. The Pharisees were jealous and envious of Jesus and had declared if any should acknowledge Jesus he would be put out of the Synagogue. The rulers enjoyed the respect, authority, and acknowledgement they received. It gave them standing, that something extra from ordinary people. If they confessed that they believed Jesus to be the Son of God, they would lose their position and reputation, they would then be treated as one of the unlearned and ignorant crowd and so they kept quiet. The praise of men was too much to lose. I wonder, were these rulers there when Jesus called the people or did they ever hear Him say whosoever shall confess me before men, him will I confess before my Father, which is in Heaven[2].

If there someone tonight who believes in Christ but you're afraid to take your stand openly on his side because of what others might say or do. You are more concerned about what people think than what God thinks. You must let nothing stop you from coming out fully on the side of Christ or you will find to your horror and dismay that because you were ashamed of Him, and denied Him before others, He will also be ashamed of you and deny you before the angels of God. Is it worth it? No. You might say, I want to come out openly for Christ but somehow, I can't. How can I? The Bible gives you the answer. Perfect love cast out fear – If you love your husband, wife, or friend, you're not ashamed to be seen with them. If you love Christ as well as believe in Him, you will be glad to acknowledge Him openly. If you are ashamed of Him, you do not love Him. Find out what is in your life that you love more than Christ. Then ask yourself, "what shall it profit a man if he shall gain the whole world and lose his own soul or be denied before God."[3]

---

[1] John 12:42-43
[2] Mark 8:34-38
[3] Mark 8:36

Broadcast 2PK   11

World Day of Prayer[1]

Do we always know exactly where to go on any trip we've taken by car? None of us can claim this, for until we've been to a place a few times and are familiar with the road, we need road maps, and often may have to ask a person along the way for directions. Unless we know where we are going, we can't possibly know the way to get there. How bewildering it must have seemed to Christ's disciples when he told them He was going to get a place ready for them in His Father's House, they knew where He was going, and they knew the way.

Let me read you a few verses from John 14:1-7

Thomas honestly questions this statement. He said, "We don't know where you are going so how can we know the way?" If He had only stated definitely where His Father's House was, they could have had some chance of knowing the way to it, but there were no definite directions or places named. But Jesus says, 'You know the way'. Not you will know it. You know the way, not you will find it as you go, but you already know the way. It seemed such a contradiction to all they felt in themselves, but is made so clear in Christ's next statements, He said, I am the way, Not I'm going the way, I'll show you the way, I AM THE WAY. He had been talking about going to the Father's House, now He says no one ever comes to the Father except by Him. If you want to find a certain street, someone gives you directions, first turn to right, past two cross streets, turn to left at next corner and so on. There is a big possibility of either hearing directions wrongly or forgetting them and so missing our way. If someone comes along and says: I live in that street come with me and I'll take you. As long as you can trust him, you don't need any directions, all you need is to stay with your friend, and he becomes the way to the street you want to find.

That is just exactly how we find our way to God, find our way through life to Heaven. Jesus says I live there. I am God, I will take you and if you only stay with Him, He will take you right through. No need of directions, no need of bewildering doubts as to whether it's the right way, or whether you'll finally reach God and Heaven.

Is there someone listening who isn't sure of your way? Are you a little fearful you just mightn't reach Heaven, are you saying I can't seem to find God? You go to church with perhaps a secret hope that you might find Him. You read articles and listen to radio sessions but somehow it doesn't seem to bring you to God. I tell you definitely today that unless the articles, sessions, sermons, and even the Bible itself leads you to Christ and you tell Him plainly where you want to go and when He says I'll take you, you're prepared to go with Him, that you will never find God. Christ is the only one who can bring you to God and however hard you try, however sincerely you pray, however devotedly you worship, it will not bring you to God without Christ, for there is no other name under Heaven given among men whereby we must be saved.

Will you stop tryngi all else and ask for Christ who is the way to God, the truth about God and the life of God.

Before I leave you, I do want to remind all the ladies of the Women's World Day of Prayer service tomorrow. This year in Parkes to be held in the Church of England of 3pm. For these 24 hours there is an unbroken chain of prayer right around the world and we do want you to share in it. Tomorrow, Friday at 3pm. Now may Christ become real to you and may you know of a certain knowledge of Christ.

---

[1] **The World Day of Prayer** is an international ecumenical Christian laywomen's initiative. It is run under the motto "Informed Prayer and Prayerful Action" and is celebrated annually in over 170 countries on the first Friday in March. The movement aims to bring together women of various races, cultures, and traditions in a yearly common Day of Prayer, as well as in closer fellowship, understanding, and action throughout the year.

Broadcast 2PK 12

Some words written as a chorus to the tune,

Don't fret nor fear when you are burdened.
There's one who cares and understands
Come unto me, all ye that labour
Ye heavy laden be at rest
For I am meek and very lowly
Learn of me, together we will bear the load
My yoke is easy, light my burden,
Ye shall find rest unto your souls.[1]

Last time I spoke to you on this session we considered the first part of this invitation of Jesus, Come unto me. Today the remainer of that invitation says, "Bend your necks to my yoke and learn from me."[2] That seems to grate, seems to be something we don't want to do.

A yoke was more familiar when these words were spoken than they are today, small bar of timber hollowed at the bottom to rest over the necks of two oxen used to pull a plow or cart.

Jesus says, come into partnership with me in my work, come learn from me, let us go together, I will teach you of God. He lived to please God. He didn't always please those around Him, but He did always please God.

Campbell Morgan says, "We say it is hard work to please God. In that view we are wrong. It is fearfully hard work to please our neighbours. It is impossible to please our friends. It is absurd to try and please ourselves. Then let the prayer of each one of us be: Teach me to do thy will O my God. That is the easiest, the sublimest, the simplest law of life and therein is best.

---

[1] Don't Sweetheart Me – (Lawrence Welk 1944)

[2] Matthew 11:28 N.E Translation

Broadcast Ayr Holiness 2PK

Mark 14:26-42

In this passage, we see a picture of Peter's confidence, a promise of loyalty, a call to fellowship in Christ's sufferings, a command and privilege to watch and pray with Him. His failure and the tragic results.

Paul, in writing to his son in the faith, Timothy, urges him to watch in all things.[1]

What are the things we must watch?

The treasure we have received, sound doctrine. Our past experience of God, reality of God's working in our lives.

We must watch our weak points. If our weak point is unbelief, pride etc. Satan will attack on that point again and again.

Watch the places where we think we are strong

"Wherefore let him that thinketh he standeth take heed lest he fall."[2]

Samson was confident that he wouldn't be taken by the Philistines, but in the end his pride led to his downfall and capture.[3]

In 1703 between 4 & 5,000 trees were blown down on an old estate when a storm came from unexpected direction. *These trees were strong, with well-established root systems. It would have seemed impossible for them to be blown down in a storm, yet they were, there is always a storm that can bring down the strongest of us, if we are not careful.* Edinburgh Castle was taken once, during all the wars in Scotland, because the Enemy came up steep rocks on the side on which they thought they were unconquerable. Showing us that the enemy can strike us in places where we never expect to be attacked from, for example, after mountain top experiences or after seasons of rich spiritual refreshment and fellowship.

Christ's temptations were following His baptism in the Jordon River when God's Holy Spirit rested on him.[4] - Elijah also had a mountain top experience on Mount Carmel and afterwards faced great fear and depression[5]

We must watch the little things. Where we would never allow some big sin to wreck our lives, quite often we are being gradually and surely weakened and overthrown by small things which are at their best, doubtful.

Pompey The Great, a Roman General, could not prevail a certain city to billet his army, but eventually persuaded them to take in a few weak and faint soldiers. These soon regained their strength and opened the gates to the entire army. He was then able to conquer the entire city. These weak and sick soldiers would have appeared to be harmless and yet they eventually brought about the downfall of the city. So it is with some trivial things in our lives that seems harmless but eventually will destroy our relationship with God.

Why must we watch? There is a time coming when many shall turn away from the truth.[6]

The enemy is so strong and subtle. We are not fighting against flesh and blood. "But know this, that if the goodman of the house had known in what watch (time) the thief would come, he would have watched, and would not have suffered his house to be broken up."[7]

Spirit is willing, but flesh is weak.[8] We damage the whole church when we fall. The nearer to the Cross we are, the fiercer the conflict, Satan aims high. He leveled his worst attacks at the Son of God.

If Christ were to come here tonight, would He find us watching as we should. We must link watching and praying together; one cannot be effective without the other.

We can be sure that Satan never sleeps, he is very wide awake, and if we are to combat evil, we must be up and doing.

How can we continually be on our Guard?

By refusing to look at the devil's temptations and attractions.

Keep our thoughts full of the things that enrich our lives, "Whatsoever things are lovely."[9]

Looking unto Jesus by prayer and finding him in the word

Satan is not asleep! If he can catch us off our guard, he gloats over a great victory.

Leave no unguarded place, no weakness in the soul. Take every virtue, every grace, and fortify the whole.

---

[1] 2 Timothy 4:5
[2] 1 Corinthians 10:12
[3] Judges 13-16
[4] Matthew 3:13-4:11
[5] 1 Kings 18-19
[6] 2 Timothy 4:3-4
[7] Matthew 24:43
[8] Matthew 26:41
[9] Philippians 4:8

Broadcast 2PK 9

15 December 1960 -2 Timothy 2:1-15

Have you used the common phrase today, 'I'll please myself what I do?' Do you feel that this is one right you possess? That of pleasing yourself. This is probably one of the most common mistakes of our day. But you say, is it a mistake? I don't have to take orders from anyone else. No, and to a degree, you are right in saying you can please yourself because God has given us a free will and we can choose one way or the other. But why did God put us here on Earth? To please ourselves? Read Revelation Chapter 4 verse11. Here we have the purpose or reason for our existence. Created for God's pleasure. Have you thought of that? Have you thought of the ways you can fulfill your purpose for living by bringing joy to God. Is he pleased with you? Can God take delight in your thoughts, conversation, feelings, actions, and motives?

It is left on record forever, the fact that a man was taken straight to Heaven without facing death because he walked with God and had the testimony that he pleased God. That man was Enoch. God said of Jesus, "This is my beloved son in whom I am well pleased."[1] Jesus gives us the secret when He said, "I came not to do my own will but the will of Him that sent me."² Again, he said, "I do always those things that please Him."³

How can we bring pleasure to God? Paul tells us! He said, "for it is God that worketh in you both to will and to do of His good pleasure."⁴

So, if you find the doing of this hard, here is a promise, it is God who will work in you, the doing of his pleasure.

If you find it hard even to be willing, this is your promise. For it is God who works in us both to will and to do His good pleasure. Here we are taught that we don't have try to please God, but simply to let God dwell in us and work in us and pleasing Him will be the outcome. This will mean a great deal of pleasure to yourself also. It is quite true that to bring happiness to someone else gives a glow of pleasure different from all others. If you bring pleasure to God there will be joy in your heart unequaled by anything else, for God Himself will be there.

But remember, God's textbook says that "without faith it is impossible to please him for He that cometh to Him must believe that He is and that He is a rewarder of them that diligently seek Him".⁵ You trust your grocer, your milkman, because if one lets you down and you can't trust him you change till you find one you can trust. Why trust God's creatures and doubt God? He said, "have I not spoken, and will I not perform?"⁶ Take Him at His word now. And ask him to work in you both to will and to do of His good pleasure.

Prayer: Lord, we thank you that it is not demanded of us that we please you ourselves, for we cannot but fail. You alone are the one who can work in us and fulfill the purpose for which you created us. Forgive us for where we have robbed you and caused you pain instead of pleasure and make us your own. Amen.

---

[1] Matthew 17:5
[2] John 6:38
[3] John 8:29
[4] Philippians 2:13
[5] Hebrews 11:6
[6] Numbers 23:19

Broadcast 2MG 1

So much is said these days about saving. We work and plan to save money. We talk about saving time. Saving energy. What really is saving?

We save money when we don't spend it on things we feel are unnecessary or less important and store it to use later for something we consider important. The same goes for time, energy, and whatever else we can think of saving. Jesus said something interesting. He that saves his life will lose it.[1] Now how does that come to be? If we save our money and never use it for anything more important, we lose it. When death takes us from earth we must part with our money, and it is lost as far as we are concerned. If we do some tasks in only half the normal time the other half can be used for something else, or we lose it. We can't store up days and years to be used at our convenience, they are lost if not used, and our energy. We might reserve our energy on certain things but unless we use it for something else it will also be lost.

What is meant by our life? He that saveth his life shall lose it. Firstly, this seems to tell me that life is given to us to use the same as all of the other gifts from God, but we can save it, not use it. Life can only be used in our contact with others in the world in which we live. It cannot help others if we never see them. If we never use our talents, gifts, powers of mind, or personality to help others, we are saving it for ourselves and what is the inevitable? We lose it. We can't store these qualities; they deteriorate and shrivel from lack of use and when life is finished so is our opportunity to use our lives and it is certainly lost forever. He that loseth his life for my sake, the same shall find it. This doesn't mean throw it away so it will never be found. We can't do that with our lives. If we spend it or use it as each day comes, we have a certain hope. But let us be careful here, there are three words we must put very heavy emphasis upon. For my sake. We can use our lives to feather our own nests, to further our own interests, Jesus gives no help of finding any return or eternal reward for that kind of spending. We shall find it only when it is spent for Him. What do you think Jesus meant by finding it. If we save it, it will be gone. If we use it, it will bring returns at the end and that return will be life at the end of this life and that only can mean eternal life. This life is in God's Son. When we give our lives to him and spend our lives for Him, He give us His life which is the life of God, eternal and everlasting. He that saveth his life shall lose it but he that loseth his life for My sake, the same shall save it. Now, the important part. Take a little time off right now. Think how you are saving for this or that. Think of your life with its possibilities for good. Think of what Jesus said and find out the answer as to what you are spending your life upon. Are you living for His sake?

---

[1] Matthew 16:25

Broadcast 2MG 2

Exodus:.19-24.

We have a major problem today – learning to live together. If only nations were at peace; countries could trade and communicate without bitterness; if states were in accord with each other; neighbourhoods on happy living terms with one another; families without strife and hatred between them; individuals really able to live together harmoniously; what a world of joy and peace we would have? But we can't live together even though God gave us the rules for such living. The last 6 of the 10 commandments tells us how to act towards our neighbours and we think of Jesus' definition of neighbour – not just the person next door but anyone we encounter. These can't be separated from the first 4 commandments because right relationships with each other depend on right relationships with God. Jesus found it essential to join them when He said, "Thou shalt love the Lord thy God with all thy heart and thy neighbour as thyself" so we dare not separate them.

Are we convinced that the 10 commandments are the rules that must govern our standard in these days? They are at least 3,500-year-old but the very fact that they have remained the basis of laws through all the century's proved their importance and practical worth. Also, we should never forget that Moses didn't find these laws written on a stone on Mount Sinai, God wrote them. Read them some time. This will help us to catch more of their real significance. We didn't make them, and we can't alter them, but we must live by them to know life as God intended. We remember through all our thinking on the 10 commandments that Jesus said that Love was the fulfilling of the law.

"Thou shalt have no other God's before me." A person's God is that to which he or she gives their highest devotion.

"Where your treasure is there will your heart be also."[1] We can find our God by taking notice of what our thoughts go to most when we're not actually concentrating on a task in hand.

Here are some examples of how other things can become our gods.

In Business: when everything revolves round how to improve, extend, increase profit, etc.

When the business is used as a ministry to those in need and carried out with integrity and honesty this is a business that is being used as God intended.

Home: if a lovely home is our only ambition, working, planning, saving to have the best in furnishings, appliances, and landscaping. Instead of these things, God would have us to open our homes to enjoy the fellowship of our fellow Christians and show the love of God to those in need.

Children: Many parents have so idolised their children or child that every spare minute goes into thinking, and planning for them. If something happens and they are taken from them they are left absolutely desolate with nothing to live for.

Do our thoughts instinctively turn to God when we are not concentrating on a particular subject. If our treasure is there – if God is first, then our heart, our affections, and thoughts will turn to Him. Then we are keeping the first commandment. Thou shalt love no god before me, or as Jesus put it, "Thou shalt love the lord thy god with all they heart and with all thy soul and with all thy mind."

---

[1] Matthew 6:21

Broadcast 2MG 3

We all know the old nursery rhyme: Pussy cat, Pussy Cat, where have you been? And it's interesting to notice that in the presence of the queen herself and all the splendour of the palace, all the pussy cat was concerned about was frightening a mouse. Why? Because he was a cat and could see only the thing that was of vital importance to him.

Someone has written another rhyme which gives us a picture of modern living:

Human soul, human soul where have you been.
In the most wonderful world that ever was seen.
Human soul human soul what did you there.
I ate and drank and had nice clothes to wear.

Human soul, human soul where have you been.
In the most sorrowful world that ever was seen.
Human soul, human soul, what did you there.
I tossed a little ball up in the air.

Human soul, human soul where have you been.
In the most purposeful world that ever was seen.
Human soul, human soul what did you there.

I went to sleep in a big armchair.[1]

Like the nursey rhyme pussy cat, it all depends on what we are ourselves, as to what we see and do in the world of ours.

In the most wonderful world, there are many human souls who are mainly interested in eating, drinking and wearing nice clothes. Is this the best for human souls when the wonders of the universe are all around us and made or our enjoyment and use?

I have recently commenced reading the Readers Digest: our human body, its wonders and its care, and I couldn't help feeling as the writers spoke of the wonders of the cell and the functioning of life which staggers ever the best brains in the world. How can we deny the existence of God, his wisdom and power?

All this and so much more is happening in and around us all the time and we are only interested in food and clothes.

In the most sorrowful world, many do not see sorrow and need, sport has become their main absorbing interesting, and they live for sport. Sport and exercise have a very necessary place in life but so has the needs of those around us as well.

In the most purposeful world, we see others giving to sleep in a big armchair. Many more don't use the armchair; they are asleep on the feet. They say we should work eight hours, and sleep eight hours but not the same eight hours. This world can be a purposeful world but as womenfolk it will depend on how we view folk.

Prayer:

I too, O Lord, would make our home a safe and lovely place.
Then teach me how for thine own sake.
To build with truth and by loves grace.
Bless thou my hands with household ways.
Help me to plan and build aright.
Teach me to sing thy praise
Within my house from morn till night.[2]

---

[1] Author Unknown
[2] Used by The Salvation Army's Home League as its prayer. By Wilhelmina Stitch, cited in Songs selected for use in Home League Meeting, (Victoria, Australia: The Salvation Army, 1961), 127.

Broadcast 2MG 4

Women's Forum

Good morning, ladies, we are glad to be able to say hello, through the medium of Radio and we hope this time together will be a benefit to someone this morning. Let us pray.

I too Oh Lord would make our home a safe and lovely place.
Then teach me how for thine own sake.
To build with truth and by loves grace.
Bless thou my hands with household way
Help me to plan and build aright.
Teach me to sing thy praise.
Within my house from morn till night.[1]

Education Week

Many mothers are visiting schools to see how their children are getting along. Education is very important and how glad we are that such a benefit is available to our children but how important is the education they get from us in our homes every day?

Psalm 119:9-16

⁹ How can a young man keep his way pure?
  By living according to your word.
¹⁰ With my whole heart, I have sought you.
  Don't let me wander from your commandments.
¹¹ I have hidden your word in my heart,
  that I might not sin against you.
¹² Blessed are you, Yahweh.
  Teach me your statutes.
¹³ With my lips,
  I have declared all the ordinances of your mouth.
¹⁴ I have rejoiced in the way of your testimonies,
  as much as in all riches.
¹⁵ I will meditate on your precepts,
  and consider your ways.
¹⁶ I will delight myself in your statutes.
  I will not forget your word.

Our learning does not end when we leave school or get through university. We can be learning all the time, and can I say, as womenfolk and mothers, we can learn such a lot from our children.

---

[1] Used as The Salvation Army's Home League as its prayer. By Wilhelmina Stitch, cited in Songs selected for use in Home League Meeting, (Victoria, Australia: The Salvation Army, 1961), 127.

1961 Christmas Breakup – Parkes

Christmas is a very busy period. Buying gifts, cooking, cleaning, Christmas parties, Christmas trees, Santa clause etc. So busy that after it is all over, we sigh and say, glad it only comes once a year.

Should we just pause and ask ourselves; *"is all this what Christmas is meant to be?"* So first we must ask what is the central fact of Christmas. Why is Christmas held every year? To celebrate and rejoice in the greatest gift God is giving to our whole world.

We thank other people for their gifts, but do we stop to thank God for the costliest of all gifts, His Son.

When one of our friends has a birthday, we try to think of something that they will enjoy, but do we even try to think what Jesus would most enjoy of all our festivity.

No matter how simple a thing, it's the love and friendship which is expressed that means most to our friends. It would mean much more to Jesus if our festivities were more simple, and done more out of love for Him on the celebration of His birthday.

In all our giving to our families, relatives, and friends, do we fail to give anything at all to the one in whose honour all this should be held?

What gift can I give Jesus that will gladden Him most? I can give to someone who is in need. I could invite someone who is lonely or unwanted to share in our rejoicings. Write to someone who is lonely and unable to come. Jesus once said, "In as much as ye have done it unto one of the least of these my brethren you have done it unto me."[1] This of course means if we do something however simple, for someone because they belong to Christ it is for Him.

But what about a gift for Himself alone. Everything we possess has come from God, so we are only giving back His own. However, we have been given a will of our own to choose what we do with money, possessions, time, and ourselves.

For us to choose to give Him these, means much to God, and the greatest we can ever give is ourselves and our love.

---

[1] Matthew 25:40

A refuge

Preached at Nambour

A refuge is a place of safety, security, and protection, where the enemy can't get us.

The air raid shelters in Brisbane were not always perfectly safe. During the war, Brisbane's line of shelters from the air would look like a line of Army supply trucks. There would always be the uncertain feeling that because that is what they looked like, they could have become a target, and a bomb might find the spot.

Places of refuge are never thought about unless there is danger, whether it's air raid shelters, lifeboats, somewhere to shelter during a lightning storm, or a child running to his father for protection. They are only considered when some danger - real, or supposed, is lurking nearby.

If there is a refuge available, it ought to be known, the way always clear, the way indicated, so when the need arises, a person knows where to go.

In Joshua we learn about the cities of refuge provided for the children of Israel. God appointed them, three each side of the Jordon River for the manslayer (someone who has committed manslaughter). He could run to a refuge city and once inside, he was safe. The tragedy of obscure directions, obstructions, and lack of knowledge of them meant that he would not be able to get justice.

The eternal God is thy Refuge[1]. David sang on the day of his deliverance from his enemies. He also sang the Lord will be a refuge for the eternal God is thy Refuge for the oppressed, a refuge in time of trouble. He found he was only really safe while in God's keeping.[2]

Let us now go back to the cities of Refuge as a type of Christ.

1 Divinely appointed: not decided by Moses or Joshua. God directed and appointed. Christ as our Refuge is divinely appointed "The father has sent me". No man-made or man appointed refuge – fulfilment of God's purposes.

2 Prominent: no city was good for refuge if it was hidden away among hills. They had to be clearly seen. Is there any more prominent figure in the world than Christ? Do as many people rely on the words of Shakespeare for the purpose of living as rely on the words of Christ? The most prominent figure in history and how is it that people shelter under the cloak of belonging to a

Christian country. Christmas is a day recognized throughout the world. Calendars date from His birth. Yes, He is central figure. Plainly seen or prominent.

3 Accessible: If set on a hill it can be seen, it's not much use to someone running for his life if there is no way to it. The drawing power of Christ Himself is the way. "If I be lifted up from the earth I will draw all men unto me."[3]

If it was not that Christ first drew me, I would never have followed. The Bible is full of signposts telling us we are on the right road or otherwise. Our conscience tells us which will lead to Christ and which away from Him. The Holy Spirit is here to testify of Christ. Yes, He can be found. This greatest of all refuges is accessible to us.

4 Universal: because a man is born in Africa means nothing in this matter. His refuge is in Christ as well as ours. Cities were not for Israelites only but also for strangers. Come unto me all, all men unto me. Not all men without exception because many have not been drawn but all men without distinction. He is the universal refuge because there is a universal need.

The names of Cities are also significant.

Kadesh – sanctuary or Holy.
Shechem – shoulder – the government shall be upon his shoulder.
Hebron – alliance – fellowship.
Bezier – Fortress.

Rayah – High place – exalted.
Golan- Joy and exultation.
All this is found in Christ.

A refuge is not provided unless there is something to escape from. Do we need to escape from our fellow men or just society. We could all become hermits but that would present problems. It would be hard to find a place far enough away from each other if we all got that idea. Escape responsibility and then we'd have to only put up with ourselves, no, nothing was ever achieved by running away. What presents the most difficulty? One person can have a poor start in life and can make good, another can have everything to start with and finish disgracefully. The difference is in the person themselves. If a man is at peace with himself, he can face anything. It's right inside of us and it's the evil within and the author, the father of evil, Satan; that's what we have to escape from. We can't run and we can't shut our eyes to it, it's there all the time. We must go to someone who can rescue us from the evil within and the one who is that evil and Jesus battled with him. Satan did his worst, but Christ could look into his Father's face and in triumph declare "It is finished!" The atonement made, Satan conquered, and in Christ Himself we can be freed, safe, protected from all his evil assaults. One condition, we must remain in Him. If we leave, Satan is outside waiting.

So, I by faith, by sin oppressed,

Would refuge take, O Christ in thee.
Thou art my hiding place and rest
From every evil shelter me.
Come away right away.
Come Jesus calls to thee.
The wounds of Christ open.[4]

---

[1] Deut 33:27
[2] 2 Sam 22:1-3
[3] John 12:32
[4] Source not found.

Acts 3:1-16

Peter and John, having witnessed the coming of the Holy Spirit at Pentecost and in the midst of revival where thousands were being saved – go with glad hearts to the temple for time apart with God.

As they approach the gate Beautiful, a cry of need reaches their ears. Should they be delayed? Did they have time to stop? What about all the others going to the temple, couldn't they give enough? Besides they didn't have any money to give him.

They stop.

This life was all that this man knew, he was born this way. I wonder how many times he looked at those around him and wanted to be able to do the things that they were doing, walking, playing, working, and having a family of his own. The man has made the plea with his head hung in shame.

In that moment it is revealed to Peter and John that his real need wasn't money; it was healing. He needed, maybe even craved, to be able to take a more active place in life, work and make his contribution to the community.

Now, with their new confidence in the power of the Holy Spirit, they know that they can give this man exactly what he needs, not what he has been settling for, for so long.

Peter is prepared to give what he had. Peter asks the man to look at him, he lifts his head with expectation, he has been noticed, how many others have just walked past him, stepped on his crippled feet, kicked him because he was in their road, looked the other way, or just threw money at him in disgust, judging him, assuming that some great sin must have been committed by his family for him to have been born with such a disability. Yet these two are telling him to look up. It feels like something very different is going on here. Then there is that moment of horror, they don't have any money to give him! Were they, too, going to be really cruel like many of the others, torturing him with hope and then snatching it away? I'm sure he held his breath, waiting for the laugh that he was sure was going to follow their declaration. Hang on, what did he say? "Get up and walk in the name of Jesus of Nazareth". He knew who Jesus was and He had passed him every time he came to the temple, he hadn't told him to get up and walk, and from what he had heard the man was dead, some people were saying that he had risen from the dead, but others insisted that his friends had stolen his body just to make out that what he had predicted had happened. Why hadn't Jesus helped him when he was here himself, and how was he supposed to do this, he'd never ever walked in his life. However, Peter was holding out his hand, he seemed willing to help him, all he had to do, it seems, was to take his hand.

Could it be that simple? If this worked, then all his dreams would be realised, he would be able to work, care for his parents, take a wife, and have a family. But this is all he knows, this has always been his life, isn't this what God expects him to do, he can't do anything else, the changes might be too scary, what if he can't actually do anything else but beg? What if he finds that he can't learn the new skills that the life he dreams of require? He must make a choice, stay where he is or reach out in faith and take that helping hand.

He takes Peter's hand and suddenly he is walking, he is jumping around, doing the things that he missed during his childhood. The man threw caution to the wind and hugged Peter and John. Oh, thank you, Lord God. Praise you for answering my prayers.

There are times in our lives when we don't understand what is going on, things look like they are going to work out, then they don't, and then they do. This man experienced all those things in a millisecond, but we often have them happen over months and even years. Yet the message here is to keep looking up, and always reach for the helping hand that is being held out to us.

If Peter had not given what he could, if they had decided that going to the temple was more important, would that man have been overjoyed at complete healing? Would God's name have been praised as it was, would the people hearing that powerful and challenging discourse from Peter been as receptive?

Later, as a result, Peter and John were put into custody by temple authorities and that could have been avoided if they had kept going, been focused on where they were headed but many who heard the word believed and the number of the men who came to faith was about 5,000.

There are several things here that relate to us today. We often ask why God doesn't answer our prayers straight away. If Jesus had healed this man on the many occasions that He had passed him, then there would have been 5000 less followers. Waiting is so often painful, it's frustrating and yet, when God does answer our prayers the results for His glory are way more spectacular than we could have ever imagined when we sent up the first prayer request.

The other important lesson for us here is to be careful about our priorities, what we think is important may just need to be delayed for a while, going to the temple to spend time with God was important but caring for the man sitting outside was more important, it was a minor detour and because they followed the leading of the Holy

Spirit, the time spent with God, while delayed was way more powerful.

Prayer: Lord, help us to be led by your Holy Spirit, to not only do the important things in life, but to be opened to the detours that will often bring you more honour and glory that we can ever imagine.

Be strong in the Lord

When we talk about someone being strong in the Lord, we think about them being endowed with **strength**[1] which might show several qualities, such as:

Stable – Firmly established, steady of purpose. David's life before he was king of Israel was filled with situations where it would have been easy to give up, but David stayed the course and trusted God.

Tenacious – Holding fast, adhesive. Job loss his wealth, health, and family but he held onto his faith in God.

Righteous – Holy, upright, just, and equitable. Joseph could have submitted to Potiphar's wife when she tried to seduce him, but he would not do what was wrong even though he was jailed for it.

Energy – Internal power to effect work. Paul had lots of energy to do the work of spreading God's word despite the challenges he faced.

Noble – Dignity of mind, high in excellence, honourable. Ruth showed dignity and excellence in her care of Naomi when it would have been easier to stay in her homeland.

Good - That which contributes to diminish pain or increase growth. Martha, Mary and Lazarus as friends of Jesus provided him with a place to stay and refresh on his journeys around Israel.

Tact - Skill in seeing exactly what to say and do in different circumstances. Mary, the mother of Jesus, showed grace in her quiet manner and her responses to the angel Gabriel.

Hardy - Bold, resolute - Peter standing up to preach after receiving the Holy Spirit, showed a boldness that he continued to employ for the rest of his life.

None of these people could have achieved what they did or stayed the course without the spirit of God in their lives. To show strength in the Lord, we must have a daily relationship with Him which fills us constantly with His power.

---

[1] These definitions are as found in Nuttall's Dictionary

Be Afternoon

We are putting the emphasis today on Being. We all know what a lot there is to do. We either have too much to do, or some complain about having nothing to do. We don't usually hear people say: "Oh dear, I have too much to be or there's nothing for me to be". Most people feel they should be more than they are. The devil doesn't like people being kind, strong, faithful, holy, and so on. So, he keeps us occupied on doing lots and lots of things and it keeps our minds off what God wants us to be.

Someone asked Jesus what shall we do that we might work the works of God? What did Jesus give for an answer? This is the work of God that you attend worship every sabbath, that you work for the church that you give all you can and so on? NO. This is what He said: "This is the work of God that ye believe on Him, whom He hath sent."[1]. What was He asking of them? Faith in Him. They didn't want to believe in Him because of all it would mean in the changes of what they were in themselves. They were doing God's service, teaching God's law but they weren't being God's people. They weren't being pure in their thinking; they weren't being good and holy in their motives and intentions.

---

[1] John 6:29

"Behold the Lamb of God which taketh away the sin of the world" (John 1:29).

Christ died on the cross so that we might be freed from our sin and its consequences. We can never pay the debt we owe.

If we were to live all the rest of our lives from now to our death, as God wants us to live, we would only be doing what we should. We can never give God more love or service then is due at any one time. So, the past can never be paid for. Through Christ's sacrifice, we can have our past forgiven. He taketh away the sin of the world. World includes you and me.

Taketh away. The Bible tells us that our sins are cast into the sea of forgetfulness. Once, a minister was much annoyed by the 'Glory", Hallelujah" 'praise the Lord' of a certain parishioner. One day the minister invited him to tea and thought to keep his mind and thoughts off praise, so gave him a book on science to read to pass the time before tea. Presently the minister was startled by a sudden outburst of Glory, Hallelujah, and Praise the Lord. "What is the matter?" asked the minister.

"Why this book says the sea is five miles deep."

"Well, what of it?"

"Why, the Bible say my sins have been cast into the depts of the sea and if it is that deep, I need not be afraid of their every coming up again."

Glory, Behold, means to look upon to observe. We must continually behold the Lamb of God. Keep our eyes fastened on Him. He is our only hope. Those of us who have looked to Him for Salvation must keep pressing on. It is dangerous to stay where we started. Gipsy Smith tells a story of a young couple with whom he once stayed. They had an only child to whom they were devoted. One night at suppertime a thud was heard on the floor of the room above. Both parents realised their little son had tumbled out of bed and hurried to the rescue. No harm, however, was done, and the next morning Mr Smith chaffingly questioned the little fellow about the noise he had heard, who, when asked why he tumbled out of bed, replied, "cos I stayed too near where I got in. We must keep looking to Jesus and follow His example and daily seek to grow more like Him and grow in grace. Those who have not looked to Jesus for Salvation, take the advice of this Bible verse found in Isaiah 45:22: "Look unto me, and be ye saved, all the ends of the earth: for I *am* God, and *there is* none else." And this hymn written by Author: Johnson Oatman.

"When you are tempted to go astray
Never lose sight of Jesus
Press onward upward the narrow way
Never lose sight of Jesus
Day and night He will lead you aright."

Being an Example

1 Timothy 4:9-12

I would like to draw your attention to the 12th verse. "Let no man despise your youth; but be an example to those who believe, in word, in your way of life, in love, in spirit, in faith, and in purity." This verse shows us that, no matter how young we are, we should be an example to those around us. We should be constantly on our guard. In our conversation we should allow nothing that is un-Christlike because once a word is spoken it cannot be taken back. It will be either for good or ill. We must also watch our actions and see that we do nothing that we would not like published. Although we may not be conscious that people are noticing us, they are constantly watching us to see if we are what we profess. This does not only apply to our Open-Air work[1] and on Sundays, but to every day of our lives. People will not read their Bibles. Thousands of people never open a Bible from one year to the next, but they read our lives, and they judge Christianity by the professing Christians they meet in their work or wherever they are. When people hear us testify in the Open-Airs they expect us to be living in accordance with what we profess. If they see us do anything that is not Christ-like, they are at once disappointed in us, and this would lower our standards in their estimation.

I read a story once of Captain Bickel, who, just before retiring to bed, met a ruffian, who had been converted, at the door on one of his journeys, Mr Bickel was tired but had a little talk with the man and asked him if he would take a Bible to a certain man the next day. The man refused saying, "No, No, Captain, he does not need that." "But why not", asked Mr Bickel? "It won't do him any good."

"But why?"

"Because it is too soon. This is your Bible and thank God it's mine now but it's not his Bible."

Mr Bickel was rather bewildered and said, "What do you mean by that!"

"Why, simply because he has another Bible, you are his Bible; he is watching you. As you fail, Christ's Fails. As you live Christ, so Christ is revealed to him".

Later when Mr Bickel was writing to his friends, he told them that he had not slept a wink that night. He had been called a liar, a thief, a spy, and many other names and had not taken much notice, but to come face to face with this was more than he could bear. As you live Christ lives, as you fail Christ fails.

I wonder how we stand today. Someone is watching us closely every day and every word we say and everything we do will be a help or a hindrance to God's Kingdom. We each have a great responsibility to God and to our fellow men.

---

[1] This refers to meetings that were held out on the street.

Quotes on Being Humble

Philip Brooks says[1]: "The true way to be humble is not to stoop until you are smaller than yourself but to stand at your real height against some higher nature that will show you what the real smallness of your greatest greatness is".

Stanely Jones[2] says: Stand at your very highest and then look at Christ and go away and be forever humble. When we lose sight of Christ, we ourselves begin to loom large.

This account says, "Jesus, knowing that the Father had given all things into His hands and that He came forth from God and goeth unto God took a towel and washed the disciples' feet."[3]

---

[1] Phillips Brooks (1835 –1893)
[2] Stanley Jones (1884–1973)
[3] John 13:3

Books and Gadgets

For Home League Mudgee/Gulgong 20/10/65

Books have been likened to people. Those we go to when we need some piece of information. Those we meet once in a lifetime. Those we think of occasionally and those we think of again and again because they really meant something to us.

Gadgets, while seeming to have no connection, are also somewhat similar. Those we use very occasionally - those that after the newness wears off, we tire of; those that are needed only for special jobs and those that are such a boon we wonder how we got on without them.

All the people that we meet in our lives will, in some way, represent all of these qualities, some will come and go, and we will hardly remember them, others will have an impact for a little while and yet others will change our lives completely.

The thing is that each person, regardless of how long they are around for, will have crossed our paths for God's own reason and we should always remember to try and show His love to them regardless of how important they may appear to be.

Children of Israel. Journey to Promised land

Ps 27 Ex 13:17-22

Pharoah was forced to let the children of Israel go.

God undertook to lead them through Moses. They were an enormous company of slaves, who had been treated as animals and given no opportunity to develop. God did not take them by the short route as probably they might have expected. Why? He had so much to teach them. His way is always best. They would have encountered exceedingly strong opposition right at the outset had they gone the short path. God had so much to teach them about His holiness, power, justice, and provision. He had to mould them into a nation. Sinai, providing food and water, the pillar of fire and cloud all would have been missed.

God is still leading his people out from the Egypt of bondage into the Canna of His fullness, which is not reached by travelling the easiest way or the quickest, there are so many lessons to learn because, not unlike the children of Israel, we forget our lessons so quickly, get weary of the struggle, and wish we could get there without so much effort.

God has a lot to do to mould us and make us fit for Heaven through discipline and refining our natures.

Their Red Sea experience could be likened to our deliverance from sin. The hosts of Satan are ready to overthrow this world. To be free from sin seems an impossibility, while we are stepping into the experience of holiness doubts assail, but God is near, lifting up the standard against the enemy, giving us the command to move forward. It is not impossible; nothing is when God is calling and leading.

To refuse to obey God and stay on the other side of the Red Sea is of course disastrous.

Then, as we travel, how are we acting? How are we responding to God's leading? Do we complain every time some little trial comes?

Do we wait for the pillar of fire and cloud or God's spirit to direct our every movement? Are we depending on God to supply us with food for our souls?

Are we as impatient as the children of Israel were or are we content to quietly wait for Him?

The first generation was not allowed to see Canaan because of their unbelief. Are we grieving God by our unbelief, and failure to count on His power?

God led his people all the way, not just past the Red Sea.

My Lord knows the way through the wilderness.[1]

"I will bring the blind by a way that they know not. I will lead them in paths that they have not known."[2]

---

[1] Sidney E. Cox 1951
[2] Isaiah 42:16

Christmas in the Home. No 3

In the first two of our series on Christmas in the Home, we have considered very briefly one or two aspects of preparing for Christmas and the sharing with others at Christmas. You are already sending parcels and receiving cards, preparing the pudding, planning holidays, rearranging things to accommodate friends and families. So, before we turn our minds for a few minutes to Christmas Day itself we'll listen to the words of O little town of Bethlehem.

How do you plan to spend Christmas day? Perhaps you are planning to go out Christmas Eve. You'll be late to bed no doubt, Santa Claus will be the reason for some early morning excitement, then the family goes to church for the Christmas service, or does mum stay home to cook the dinner? Then what? Do you sleep it off, visit friends, go driving, there's numerous things you could do. Does it really matter that much what you do? Perhaps, more important, is why you plan to spend it the way you do. I often think we are so concerned with what we do that we forget to ask why we do things. Are we planning Christmas Day because we want a good day? Do we want a holiday? A day when we don't have to go to work and can please ourselves what we do and so we could take two little words with two letters each, and letter two is the same in each word. Could you guess them? I'll tell you. HE and the other is ME. Now have you ever tried to have a birthday celebration without the person concerned being present? Think about it for five minutes and you will be convinced that it just wouldn't be the same. How many of Christ's birthdays have you tried to celebrate with scarcely even passing Him a thought and so He is left out and Me becomes the chief concern. What do I want to do? Where would I like to go? What can I have that I would really enjoy? Does this mean that unless I look after myself and see that I have a good time, I must go round with a long face all day. He wants us to enjoy the celebration of His birth for didn't the angel say I bring you tidings of great joy? And didn't Jesus Himself say after He had been speaking to His disciples about abiding or dwelling in Himself, these things have I spoken unto you that My joy might remain in you and that your joy might be full?

Of course, if you only have religion and a form of dos and don'ts, you won't enjoy Christmas by making it a religious day. Someone has said that going to church doesn't make you a Christian any more than going to a garage makes you a motor car, but you can look for Christ through the church in so many other ways. He can reveal Himself. John says "He that committeth sin is of the devil for the devil sinneth from the beginning. For this purpose, the Son of God was manifested that He might destroy the works of the devil."[1]

This is a wonderful Christmas message, for this was when Jesus was manifested, when He became flesh and dwelt among us. What for? To destroy the works of the devil. What is it that causes wars, and untold sorrows throughout the world? James tells us this is a result of lust and greed.[2] What causes unhappiness in the Home? Isn't it selfishness, jealousy, and all these things that are the work of the devil?

But Jesus was born, lived, died, and rose again that He might destroy these things and bring righteousness, peace, and joy. If you let Christ destroy selfishness, greed, covetousness, pride, and all the other things that don't honour God and put your life under His control, then joy will be in you and, with Jesus in the family, it's a happy, happy home. Someone has taken the very familiar Christmas tune of jingle bells and written words that can really spell joy for you this Christmas.

"J O Y, J O Y, This must surely mean, Jesus first, yourself last and others in between." If you honour the Lord, this is what you will do.

Prayer: Dear Father, lead us to find Christ, to put Him first, others next and ourselves last. Help us to pray sincerely the words we heard earlier.

---

[1] 1 John 3:8
[2] James 1:15

Christmas in the Home. No. 5

A listener has suggested that this series be carried on for the two remaining weeks till Christmas. I feel it would give us the opportunity to think about two other aspects of this subject. Tonight, we could give some time and thought to those who are not looking forward to a happy Christmas, in fact, not looking forward to Christmas at all, because, since last Christmas, a loved and familiar face has gone from them. Perhaps it is some years ago and Christmas time with its family reunions always brings with it a keen awareness of sorrow and loss.

Could I read you a poem written by a Mrs E V Wilson about one such lady, The title: Lady Judith's Vision.[1]

This poem tells of a mother who is so grief stricken over the death of her son, that she refuses to participate in any Christmas festivities until a vision shows that her son is sad in Heaven because she cannot move on with her life. He begs Jesus to let him return to earth so he can comfort his mother, leaving behind the beauty and joys of paradise. Jesus is about to grant his request when the mother realises what he would be giving up for her and begs him to stay. Instead, she fills her life by helping those poor children who do not have parents to care for them, knowing that by doing so, her son will also be rejoicing in Heaven.

Instead of sitting down in her grief and allowing bitterness to creep in, with a change of vision she was able to really make Christmas for so many Children who had never seen half of what she was used to every day. What a pity if she had spent the day locked in her room overwhelmed by her own loss and sorrow. If Christmas will mean heartache for you, perhaps you could ask God to show you how you could turn that very loss into gain for His kingdom and joy to someone else. Sorrow, loss, and disappointment will come to us all sooner or later. What comes to us is not as vital as what we do with what comes. Like Lady Judith they can be stepping stones to greater usefulness and a fuller life.

---

[1] This poem is too long to insert here so the author has summarised it as follows. The original was published in Cheery Comedies for Christmas, 1915.

Cleaning the Temple – Mark 11:1-19

Early in the morning the day after the triumphal entry, Jesus went straight to the Temple. He cleansed it of all money lenders and traders and then stood guard. Verse 16: *"And would not suffer that any man should carry any vessel through the temple."* (and would not allow anyone to carry merchandise through the temple courts. NIV) How could Jesus close His eyes to this when He had come to set up His Father's Kingdom. This was God's chosen house where His people met and worshipped Him.

We are the temple of God. When we come to Jesus for salvation, our hearts and lives will be cleansed, He cleans it out but then He stands guard over it as we continue to serve him.

Judgment must begin at the House of God. If God's own people fail Him, they will be judged according to their light and understanding. Christ has every right to expect holiness and purity in His temple. How tragic it is for Him to find it polluted by sin.

Verse 17, Jesus declares *"My house shall be called of all nations the house of prayer?"*

Prayer means fellowship, praise, desire towards God, worship. We are created for this purpose. We should ask ourselves "Are our hearts kept only for this purpose?" Or have we opened it to some other traffic making it a Den of Thieves robbing us of our fellowship with God.

What are the things in our lives that rob us of our fellowship with God?

Doubt, wanting for this world's gain, worldliness, not being able to let go of the hurt that is caused by a slight from other people, misunderstandings, or discouragement.

Jesus put all the traders outside the place. He did not allow them to stay and just forbid trade, He was not only suppressing them but rooting them out. Christ and evil cannot abide together. He keeps His temple clean.

Crusade Home League Dubbo   1964

Held.

Only a small word, but how much it conveys, what pictures it could bring to our minds. Often, we don't appreciate the fact that we can hold things until we see someone who hasn't the power to hold. We can think of a baby being held and all that this means. A toddler being held when learning to walk. A child being held when frightened. All through our lives we hold many things, some of us even get to holding hands. As the years roll by, we will need someone to hold us as our steps falter and we become feeble. Some things are held to our own hurt, like firecrackers,[1] they explode and burn us. Some mothers selfishly hold to their children, instead of letting them make another independent home unit and have caused a lot of unhappiness. However, some things must be held, and we let them go to our own hurt. We can't hold on to material things beyond this life and often not even for long in this life. Three things can be held and must be held unless we are to lose everything, Faith, hope, and love.

Faith, "without faith it is impossible to please God."[2]

Hope. God did this so that, by two unchangeable things in which it is impossible for God to lie, we who have fled to take hold of the hope set before us may be greatly encouraged. [3]

Love, "love worketh no ill to his neighbour therefore love is the fulfilling of the law."[4]

"And now abideth faith, hope, and love."[5] These things must be held firmly in our personal living, our marriage, our family, and our community.

Sometimes we feel like my six-year-old when he climbed halfway up a pepper tree after a bird and couldn't get down. As he held on, and we guided him down he weaken a few times and panicked. "I'm going to fall; I can't hold on!' Often, we feel we can't hold on to righteousness, goodness, faith, hope, or love any longer and here is where God has a message for us. "I the lord, will hold thy right hand saying unto thee, fear not, I will help thee."[6] It is God who is the Giver and source of righteousness, goodness, faith, hope, and love. It is then God, through these things, that holds us.

Does He really hold us? "I give unto them (those that hear His voice and follow Him) eternal life and they shall never perish neither shall any man pluck them out of my hand."[7] He will hold us if we let him.

How does He hold us? By supplying us with a source of knowledge. Many a motorist has been held to the right road by a knowledge of the route and a map. Many a girl (or young person) has been kept in safety by a knowledge of the dangers. If we know the right way to live and the dangers that await us, it will be our safety if we follow directions. God not only gives us the directions, He comes Himself, in the person of His Holy Spirit, to abide in us, to prompt us, to restrain us, to give wisdom, encourage us, and to interpret the guide book to us.

Next time someone asks you just to hold this or that for them, or you hold someone to save them from falling, let your mind go to the things you must hold, righteousness, goodness, faith, hope, and love, then think of the things you must not hold, grudges, selfishness, envy, pride etc. but make sure your mind then goes to the One who has promised to hold you and say to yourself, "Who shall separate us from the love of Christ? Shall trouble or hardship or persecution or famine or nakedness or danger or sword? As it is written:

"For your sake we face death all day long; we are considered as sheep to be slaughtered. No, in all these things we are more than conquerors through him who loved us. For I am convinced that neither death nor life, neither angels nor demons, neither the present nor the future, nor any powers, neither height nor depth, nor anything else in all creation, will be able to separate us from the love of God that is in Christ Jesus our Lord."[8]

There is a danger of turning your focus on yourself and forgetting that Jesus said, "without me ye can do nothing."[9]

Could I say that this is one of the biggest dangers Salvationist women and indeed Christian women face. Satan has kept women in many countries in a position of inferiority, but when, by God's leading and power, they gain the place of victory and usefulness, Satan then tries to push us too far to where we feel that so much depends on us.

Devotion to duty and the work of God is not an acceptable substitute for devotion to Christ. If devotion to duty and the work of God is an outcome of devotion to Christ then it is acceptable to God, if not our real devotion centres around ourselves and the desire to be needed and important.

What must we do that we might work the works of God? Was a question put to Jesus. His reply, "this is the work of God that ye believe on Him whom He has sent"[10], and in another place, He said, "Why call ye me Lord, Lord, and do not the things that I say."[11] To really believe on Him as the son of God is to obey His commands. He is not Lord if we take no notice of what He says. When we are on the path of obedience then we can expect His protection and guidance. Brigadier Enid Lee, a missionary in Malaysia in the days when it was dangerous to be a Christian there, was being searched for by terrorists and I'm sure that she was confident in that she could say, "I know He cares for me. I'll Trust my Heavenly Father for I know that He cares for me."

---

[1] This refers to small fireworks that were allowed at the time.
[2] Hebrews 11:6
[3] Hebrews 6:18
[4] Romans 13:10
[5] 1 Corinthians 13:13
[6] Isaiah 41:13
[7] John 10:28
[8] Romans 8:35-39

[9] John 15:5
[10] John 6:29
[11] Luke 6:46

Cups

Such useful little objects, big ones, used by the man of the house, pretty ones for show, plain ones for hard work, unbreakable ones for babies, enamel or tin for bushmen. As the number of types of cups vary so does the manner of using them. Babies grab with both hands, men just drink from them without fuss, some women think it tastes much nicer if the little finger is at the right angle, but however they are used, it is perhaps the most popular piece of crockery we have. First of all, we think of a broken cup - not a scrap of use. Sticking plaster is useless, the only thing to do is to throw it in the rubbish. However, a master of Kintsugi could take all the pieces and put it back together with precious metals, making it more beautiful than before. A broken life is useless unless in the hands of the One who designed and made it and if He has all the pieces, he will make it over anew.

If you go to a Café, and you are daintily served with a cracked cup you are horrified. It isn't fit for any place of honour, and it may not have been much of a bump that did the damage. Cracks come in so many lives, things that mar, little grievances when someone has bumped us.

A dirty cup is the greatest insult. We can see why it is such an insult to God if we are dirty inside. Outside might look alright but the inside counts most and God looks on the heart. To truly be clean, we must be really cleaned out by God. A cup can't clean itself.

From all your filthiness and from all your idols will I cleanse. If we confess, cleanse us from all unrighteousness.

A clean cup doesn't have to be flash, but it does have to be clean. This is the first step to being useful. So, we can pray with the Psalmist, "Create in me a clean heart Oh God"[1], and if we really mean it, He will do just that. It is a new creation, a full cleaning out of sin and evil thoughts and desires.

If you were dying of thirst, a cup, however clean, is just a taunt unless it has some water in it. If our lives are empty, then we are unable to assist those who come to us for encouragement. A cup that is full cannot receive anything else unless it is emptied out. We can follow Jesus' example and empty ourselves, looking not to our own interests but the interests of others.[2] If we are 'full of ourselves', there is no room to receive anything, from God or others. What is inside will spill out under stress or disruption, so we should fill our lives with "…. whatsoever things are true, whatsoever things *are* honest, whatsoever things *are* just, whatsoever things *are* pure, whatsoever things *are* lovely, whatsoever things *are* of good report; if *there be* any virtue, and if *there be* any praise, think on these things."³

---

[1] Psalm 51:10
[2] Philippians 2:4
[3] Philippians 4:8

Dolls

There seems to be no end to the variety of dolls available. There are ones that look like babies, ones made from rubber or plastic, teddy bears, animals, national dolls, barbie dolls, mama, walking, sleeping, bed dolls, to name a few.

There is a greater variety in people because, unlike the dolls, there are no two people exactly alike.

National dolls are interesting not only to children but adults as well, not because it's a doll but because of how it is dressed. Say you were of Dutch descent, living in Australia, and you saw a Dutch doll in a shop window. It would catch your interest because its costume evokes memories of what was once your home.

People are interesting, there is usually something about the other person we haven't yet discovered. When we engage with people, they are always coming up with interesting bits about themselves that we didn't know but we only find out if we take the trouble to appreciate and look for them.

Some dolls are highly valued, not because they're so expensive but because of their sentimental value. That might depend on who gave it to us, or the many hours we spent playing with it or all the other things we've done with them. A doll is ours, not usually shared with someone else. It no surprise how sad we feel if someone steals or breaks our doll.

We are valued by God; we are His own. He loves us. Can you imagine how sad God is when the devil ruins us by sin and robs Him of His treasured child.

Factories make many dolls exactly alike but when they go to their different homes they soon become quite different, but God has made every single person uniquely different, so with all the millions upon millions, no two people are exactly the same and this makes people so interesting and shows how great God is, when each person has two eyes, a nose and mouth that go in approximately the same place and yet we're different and he loves us, we mean a lot to Him. He hasn't made another exactly like us in every detail and He wants us to be the kind of person He planned, to love and worship Him and give Him pleasure. God knows how hard the devil tries to stop this, Paul said, "I can do all things through Christ which strengthens me."[1] so God can be pleased with you and me through Jesus who is not only our Saviour but our best friend.

---

[1] Philippians 4:13

Five Senses

We have all heard of common sense, which, on the whole, is very uncommon. There's horse sense, nonsense, and just plain sense but our five senses are very different.

Sight, Hearing, Touch, Taste, and Smell. We are certainly fearfully and wonderfully made.

Sight: In order for us to see there are two little balls inside our head, some are blue, some brown, some other colours yet what important little things they are. What an everyday thing to say, I saw… It's amazing what we see sometimes and just as amazing what we don't see even though we look straight at it. Oh. 'I see' is used when we understand. Can't you see? Some exasperated informer asks when we are just too dull to take it in.

What kind of things do we see? Two men looked through prison bars, one saw mud the other saw stars.

"Blessed are the pure in heart for they shall see God."[1]

Hearing: One of the things we hear is the Wireless. Sometimes we wish we couldn't hear some of the neighbours' wirelesses. Sometimes it is much better if we don't hear all that comes over our own. Often, we don't hear what we should because we are not interested enough. "There is none so deaf as those who that will not hear".[2] Johnny playing down the street becomes suddenly deaf when mum calls him in for tea and Mary really didn't hear mum tell her to do the washing up.

Jesus gave good advice, "take heed what ye hear."[3] We can be so busy listening to all the noise around us that we miss the very best.

He came to you, for in His gentle voice
He'd much that He would say …
Your ears were turned to earth's discordant note
And so … He went away.[4]

I'm listening in, are you?

Touch: We do like to touch. Children in big stores want to handle everything. A touch can harm when we meddle. A touch can help. The woman who touched the hem of Christ's garment. The master touch healed her. A child was frightened by the whirl of some machinery; her father touched the switch, and, in a moment, the whole thing ceased its terrifying noise. Just as Jesus went about touching those who were in distress and need, bringing to them the love of God, our touch can help and bless and lead others to Him.

"Down in the human heart, crushed by the tempter,
Feelings lie buried that grace can restore;

Touched by a loving heart, wakened by kindness,
Chords that are broken will vibrate once more."[5]

Taste: I'm sure every mother of very small children has cried, why must everything go to their mouths. Most of us can tell what something is by its taste. When we are sick, often food tastes queer and therefore unappetising, taste helps us to have a good appetite. Sometimes we make up our mind we don't like a thing and yet with a bit of perseverance we acquire a taste for it. The best remedy is to be starving and we'd eat it whether we wanted to or not. German children were reported as having to eat potato peelings during the war.

There's a saying, the test of the pudding, is in the eating. "Oh, taste and see that the Lord is good."[6]

Smell: Some smells are lovely, some not so much. Once we had the misfortune to have some animal die under the hall. The next Sunday, Major spoke on smells. The trouble was that was very hard to get rid of it.

The Fragrance of a flower is a wonderful thing, particularly when we are able to smell it and appreciate it.

"If I've Jesus, Jesus only. I possess a cluster rare. He's the lily of the valley and the Rose of Sharon fair."[7]

Prayer: Make my heart a garden so that flowers may grow, shedding heavenly beauty in this world below.

Jesus thine own fragrance by the love impart, lily of the valley bloom, within my heart.

---

[1] Matthew 5:8
[2] Matthew Henry
[3] Mark 4:24
[4] Jim Binney
[5] Rescue the Perishing verse 3, Fanny Jane Crosby 1820-1915
[6] Psalm 34:8
[7] Jesus Only, Hattie M Conrey 1877

God is Love

1 John 4:7-21

One of the shortest and yet one of the greatest and most profound texts in Scripture is found in this passage. "God is love". God's great love is something not one of us can explain, but it is gloriously possible for every one of us to experience. When we look through the pages of God's word, right from beginning to end, we see written largely the fact that God loves us. The realization of this brings instantly from our hearts the question, "Why should God love me?"

In our earthly wisdom and pride, we think we have a right to love only the lovable people and those who love us, but "God commended His love toward us in that while we were yet sinners, Christ died for us."[1] While we were setting ourselves against God, living in rebellion, deliberately breaking His laws, and while we were in the clutches of Satan, God loved us as no human ever has or ever will love us.

When we were half-hearted, when we didn't care how God felt about our doings and didn't love Him. We were ashamed to be known as a follower of Christ. "Ashamed of Jesus? Yes, I may when I've no sin to wash away. No tears to wipe, no good to crave, and no immortal soul to save"[2].

He still loved us when we wounded Him by doubting His love and wisdom, when we belittled Him by saying we couldn't be saved or kept, which is another way of saying that God has not the power to do so.

How is His love manifested to us?

He sends His spirit to reveal our sin and warns us of coming disaster. Just as a mother out of love for her child warns about the dangers around them, such as stranger danger, His Holy Spirit quickens our desires for higher way of life. His word explains to us the way of Salvation, our obligations to God, and the way of Holiness. It explains how God sent His son to make an atonement or to reconcile and bring us into a state of friendship and oneness with God and each other. Would anything but love prompt the making of such a sacrifice. Having provided the way, He does not leave us to get there the best way we can, but gives us power. "To as many as receive Him, to them gave the power to become the sons of God."[3]

He then fills us with His Holy Spirit. With the spirit of God dwelling in our hearts, we need have no fear of defeat. Just like the story of a King who presents a jewelled cup to a soldier. The soldier's response is "This is too great a gift for me to receive" but the King replies, "It's not too great for me to give." God's answer to us is the same.

Surely, when we are completely filled with the love that God gives us, we will be convinced that God's love surrounds us, and it is His deepest longing that we should be free from sin and completely lost in Him.

Have we been drawn by that amazing love? How much have we allowed Him to fill our lives?

---

[1] Romans 5:8
[2] Timothy 1:8
[3] John 1:12

Good Work

"Being confident of this, that he who began a good work in you will carry it on to completion until the day of Christ Jesus."[1] There were some things about which Paul was very sure of and this is one. He was confident of this very thing. This good work began by God.

God's hand began its good work. Work of highest good for ourselves, for us an exceeding weight of glory. Bringing us to a place of fitness for fellowship and preparing us for Heaven.

Good work for sake of others. Blessing and light brought to others because Christ is living in us.

Good work because of His own name and glory. God chooses to glorify His name through human lives and by doing this wonderful work of grace, saving, seeking His own in the world by His great power, and amazing love.

It began first by a revelation. It may be startling or gradual awareness of our need for a saviour. It may be as children we felt we wanted to be good and needed help. It may be that we saw the sins rising like great mountains that simply defied very attempt at peace or reform and we needed forgiveness. It may be that we felt the need of a friend and companion to share life's secrets and problems. However, it came to bring us to realize we had a need, and that need was for Christ. The work went on, we were sorry for all our sinful misdeeds, sorry for having hurt the one who loved us.

His work only began when he helped us to see our next and important step, the bringing of our all to the light. Open confession of a personal longing and expectancy for forgiveness. God in his mercy forgave. The load lifted, and joy and peace came. We want to please Him, we want to tell others, but we feel weak. There is still a tendency toward bad temper and the sting of pride. We don't love as we know God requires, we feel generally that we are failing. Satan says we are not saved, we know God saved us, but self has a big demand and like the song writer said. "Can I never be free from this dreadful bondage within, comes a longing to be pure, free and united to Him?"[2]

This is all God's work, and He continues. If we are to really have victory and lasting peace there must be a complete surrender. Here the battle begins, self will not let go easily, Satan does his worst. We want all that God brings but we ask, 'haven't we a right to a little of this or that?' Ambition, desire, a cherished friend, an indulgence, but God knows it must be all. We must be willing for them all to go if He desires it that way. Just be willing for God to take over. God does not give up but pleads that we let go of these temporary and harmful things and then we must decide. Since I gave my all to Jesus, Jesus gives himself to me.

"But He called me closer to Him, bade my doubts and fears all cease, and when had fully yielded, filled my soul with perfect peace."[3]

The work is not all done yet. He will perform it until the day of Jesus Christ's return. Every day we must learn, He shows how we can do His will, He supplies power, He gives guidance, encourages, refines, strengthens, and develops until the day we stand before our Father.

---

[1] Philippians 1:6
[2] Salvation Army Hymn Whiter Than the Snow
[3] Once I thought I walked with Jesus F A blackmer 1855-1930

Harvest Thanksgiving 18th March 1951

Ps. 65, 1 Chron 29:10-14

"For all things come of thee and of thine own have we given thee." Verse 14.

In his thanksgiving for the building of the Temple, David acknowledges that God had given everything and therefore they were only giving back what belonged to Him. At this season of thanksgiving for God's goodness, let us consider:

God's gifts

Temporal Blessings – Sunshine, rain, fresh sir, food, flowers, home, and loved ones.

Physical blessings – our own health, strength, intelligence, senses of sight, hearing, and smell.

Spiritual blessings – Salvation, peace of mind and heart, companionship with God, the presence of the Holy Spirit, opportunity to work for and with Him.

Outcome of His love - When we think of the boundless measure of His gifts to us, we realize something of the love He has for us. He could give us the mere essentials and we still would have cause to thank Him, yet He loads us with benefits.

He doesn't give according to what we deserve. If He did, we would not only be deprived of the beautiful and sweet things of life but would constantly be under condemnation and punishment.

Our attitude to God's Gifts

Almost without fail, we accept His benefits as if we had every right to receive them, as though it is his duty, rather than an act of grace. We take them for granted and seldom, if ever, even stop to think where they came from and who give them.

We are always crying for something we think we need and forget to thank Him for all we have.

With every little mishap or trouble, we immediately blame God and wonder why He should deal so harshly with us. Next time we feel like this, let us stop and think how we have treated God. Think how little time, thought, money, goods, or anything else we have been willing to give to Him or His service.

What can we give Him in return for his mercy?

If we only give Him a certain amount of money or other possessions, we can see how poor a return it is for His love, because all that we possess belongs to God already.

God knows we can never pay the debt we owe but He expects us to be grateful. We are usually very careful to show earthly friends our gratitude when we receive a gift or kindness from them. Is our Father in Heaven less worthy of thanks than they. How it must grieve Him for us to never to give a word of thanks. Try thanksgiving.

Widow's mites[1]. Many make this story an excuse for their small giving. I will give my mite. The widow's mites were all that she had. How much better off the kingdom would be if they would give their mites to the same value that the Widow gave, all that they have?

Jesus measures our gifts not by what we give but by what we have left. What it cost us. Ours will not be true gratitude unless it means giving our all. Jesus did not despise the widow's little gifts, because they were all that she had.

---

[1] Luke 21:1-4

Holiness

The purpose of 'Holiness Meetings', is to lead our people into an experience of Holiness and help them in the life of Holiness.[1] We each, this morning, are longing to live the life of holiness to the highest, not to satisfy ourselves, or to convince others we are good people but to please God. Every sin wounds the heart of God; therefore, we can't bring pleasure to Him if we are to go on sinning and repenting all our lives.

When I came to God, I was concerned with all the things I'd done wrong and asked God to forgive. I didn't stop to think that sin went very much deeper than telling a lie or being angry. As the days went by, I found I was very selfish, even desires to be good were to satisfy my love of praise. One day was alright, the next I would be fighting against an evil feeling and it would get the better of me. Then despair of never being victorious. I wasn't living just for God alone. I wanted God as long as it suited the way I felt.

Every person that's been really saved gets to the place where they feel that if they are really to win through and live a true Christian life, something must be done. Here God reveals the blessing of holiness.

It shows its possible for me. We believe in it because others say that God has freed and cleansed and indwelt them. This can be different when it comes to our own hearts where we know something of what has to be conquered. To say that God can't make and keep me holy is to belittle God not myself. If I'm not being freed, it's because I won't let Him, not that He can't do it. Why did He make me see I needed something more and create a longing for that experience if it wasn't for me?

"Be ye holy"[2], is as much for every Christian now as when it was written.

If it is for me, then do I possess it? Possessing holiness means being cleansed from all unrighteousness and being wholly given over to God for Him to do with us whatever He wants.

As the chorus says: "'tis glorious to know the barriers are broken and gone; Wherever He leadeth there gladly I'll go, For Jesus and I are at one. Jesus with me is united, Doubtings and fears are all gone, With Him now my soul is delighted, Jesus and I are at one'.[3]"

Holiness is practical otherwise it is useless for everyday circumstances. Holiness prepares a way for the fullness of God's love, perfect peace, hearty agreement with God's will, and readiness to witness.

---

[1] Historically, The Salvation Army would have a meeting dedicated to the preaching and teaching of holiness each week. Usually during the Sunday

morning meeting (church service). At times there would also be a monthly mid-week holiness meeting in the evening when a number of Corps (Churches) would gather together for teaching on Christian holiness.

[2] 1 Peter 1:16

[3] Chorus from The Salvation Army Song by Herbert H. Booth. Titled "One with my Lord!"

How committed are you?

I came across this message, and I hope this abridged version will encourage and challenge us. The message is based on Daniel 3.

1   Idols.

Idolatry is giving worship due only to God to something else. It need not be gold, wood, or stone, it can be money, education, business pleasures, companions, art, music, or home. These are perfectly right in their place but become sin when put in place of God. God must come first.

A church girl, defending her practice of attending places of amusement, said to her minister, 'I take Christ with me to the theatre and dance hall.' The minister quietly replied: 'Indeed, is that so? You can take Jesus with you. I did not know that was the order, that it was yours to lead and His to follow'. Christ is our leader, and he commands us to renounce the world. So, we cannot be a follower of Him if we are not willing to do as he commands. We are told to love the Lord with all our heart.

2   The three men had five things that were important.

1: Had a strong conviction. They knew in whom they had believed.

2: Faith. Our God is able.

3: Steadfastness. They were not as a wave driven with the wind.

4: Courage. They gave a bold testimony before the king.

5: Love. Nothing but love would induce them to take such a stand.

Love must be our ruling force. They proved God's power not only in the furnace but in temptations prior to it. This world is in desperate need of courageous men, women, and children who will stand up for 'right', whatever happens.

3   Furnace

A bold confession will undoubtedly lead to a furnace. The Hebrews were warned of their fate. As Christians, we are told that we will have tribulation, so it's no use saying it wouldn't come to that. Trial and persecution cannot be escaped by any Christian who boldly declares himself. Many professing Christians are so lukewarm that the devil knows they will never do his kingdom much harm. He knows too, that with Christ's power within us, we can be a very dangerous enemy to his ranks. Christ also suffered at the hands of sinners and religious leaders.

4   What made the difference in this story?

Nebuchadnezzar received three shocks.

Firstly, the three fell down into the middle of this terrible furnace when his men were killed at the entrance by the intense heat.

Secondly, the men got loose and were walking calmly about.

Thirdly, he saw the form of a fourth man which was like the son of God. He made sure that only three had been thrown in.

The big difference was that God was there. What a great moment for these men. God's presence was so real to them. They were true to Him and He never failed them.

Perhaps we are having a bad time. Trouble and temptations seem to overwhelm us. Without God, even the smallest and most trifling circumstances will prove disastrous but with God all the powers of Satan cannot harm us. The harder the fight, the more glorious the victory. The most important thing is to have God's spirit in our lives.

Let us take fresh courage and remember these men of faith who triumphed in God's strength. God is stronger than His foe:

Lord, I Believe

Three words – God – Me – Faith

We are inclined to emphasize the wrong end of this phrase. A Woman known as one of great faith, when asked by a visitor, she replied, "no, I am the woman with a faith in a great God". We often think of our faith and wish we had more and forget the great God on whom we should be depending.

The First Word: 'Lord'. If He doesn't come first, then we don't really believe in Him. If we do not crown Him Lord of all, we do not crown him Lord at all. Jesus said, "all power is given unto me in Heaven and in Earth"[1]. If we say we believe Him, believe what He says, then why are we so powerless? He says, "My grace is sufficient for thee, for My strength is made perfect in weakness"[2], then why do we get so frustrated and beaten by circumstances? So, God goes on promising all we need to live so as to please Him, all we need to fit us for Heaven, and we go on saying we believe Him and all the time we are uncertain, discontented, fearful, and weak. The three Hebrew boys of Daniel's day said with confidence, "Our God is able"[3], and our God is still able to do exceedingly abundantly above all that we ask or think"[4].

The Second word: 'I'. Others believe God, our mothers in many cases did, people of all races do, but that is of no benefit to us unless we believe personally. The ten disciples believed Jesus has risen from the dead, but however hard they talked to Thomas, their faith didn't make him happy. Only when he had personal contact with Christ was he convinced, and the cry "My Lord, and my God"[5] was his own heart's cry. Do we believe Christ to be the head of the church, the saviour of the world, and yet, must confess that, when it comes to our own private life, personal plans, and decisions, He's not always asked to control? He may be sometimes, but at other times it is too inconvenient. When it comes to giving our lives completely as they are, with home, loved ones, possessions, everything to Christ, do we say, "Thy will, not mine, be done."[6]

The Last word: 'Believe'. A Faith Songwriter puts it "There is confidence in Him who holds us"[7]. Not enough to say we believe, because the devils also believe and tremble.[8] It must be more than that. It must be a confidence brought about by personal experience of God's faithfulness. We all have a friend somewhere that we really trust. Why? Because we've been in some circumstances where they've proved themselves, and we'd continue to believe in them until they let us down. If they never do, then they are worthy of the trust we have placed in them. If they promise us something, we act on it and prove for ourselves whether or not they are dependable. How can we prove God to be trustworthy and absolutely dependable if we never act on His promises, if we never take Him at His word?

But without faith *it is* impossible to please *him*: for he that cometh to God must believe that he is, and *that* he is a rewarder of them that diligently seek him."[9] Take his promises, look up to Him and say; Lord I Believe, prove it by acting on His word, then "according to your faith it shall be done unto you."[10]

A small boy was travelling in a bus from Sunday School proudly holding a card on which was printed the words, Faith in God', when a sudden wind caught it and carried it out of the window. The driver and passengers were rather amused to hear a little voice from the back of the bus shouting, 'Stop the bus, I've lost my faith in God.' As the journey proceeded the smiles on many faces changed to more serious expressions as they realized that they had really lost their faith in God.

---

[1] Matthew 28:18
[2] 2 Corinthians 12:9
[3] Daniel 3:17
[4] Ephesians 3:20
[5] John 20:28
[6] Luke 22:42
[7] Australian SA officer Lily Sampson, "As the varied way of life we Journey", The Song Book of The Salvation Army, (London, UK: SP&S, 1953), 740
[8] James 2:19
[9] Hebrews 11:6
[10] Matthew 9:29

Love our Enemies.

How do we go about doing this? Here are some ideas.

Don't judge others by what they do and say. God alone knows their motive, reason, and specific circumstances. His is the only judgement that is fair.

Christ does not demand something unreasonable and impossible because He tells us that He loved us even though we ignore Him and His blessings on our lives, which is the same as being His enemies.

God is kind to the unthankful (and one of the hardest things to take is ingratitude) and the evil because He sends rain on both those who love Him and those who don't.[1]

Help those who hate us.

Pray for the best for those who wish harm to us.

Pray for any who do low and mean things to us.

If anyone slaps us across the face, which could be a situation where someone insults you, turn the other cheek as instructed by God in the Bible "But I say unto you, That ye resist not evil: but whosoever shall smite thee on thy right **cheek**, **turn** to him the **other** also".[2] A Christian's response might be: refraining from insulting them back, saying something kind instead, asking them for more insults and praying for them?

Wisely help all who come asking for assistance without expecting anything in return.

Treat everyone as you expect to be treated.

---

[1] Matthew 5:45
[2] Matthew 5:39

Men seek better methods; God seeks better men.

"The Spirit of the Lord *is* upon me, because he hath anointed me to preach the gospel to the poor; he hath sent me to heal the broken hearted, to preach deliverance to the captives, and recovering of sight to the blind, to set at liberty them that are bruised,"[1]

God is continually seeking better men but how will He find them? He knows, and so do we, that we will never become better people unless He makes us such. Haven't we tried to improve, haven't we tried to be better? Haven't we fretted because the more we try and struggle the worse we seem to become?

Men try to improve conditions, environments, everything, but miss the central thing, the heart of man, but mankind has gone from bad to worse.

God came down, not to *find* better men so much as to *make* better men.

At Christmas we see how He came, and we see how His first visitors were better men for having met and worshipped the Christ.

We know how he came, where He was born, and so much connected with this great event, but why did He come?[2]

He was anointed to preach the gospel to the poor, did He make better men in this regard? We look at the cross and He is almost alone. How many were changed by his preaching the gospel of the kingdom? Look down the ages, how many have been changed by hearing and reading what Jesus preached when He was here in physical form?

He was sent to heal broken hearted. How many despairing souls have found hope because Jesus loved them. Because He stopped, stooped, and healed those who were crushed by circumstances, sorrow, trouble, broken in spirit, with nothing to live for. There is a glorious change because Jesus came to make better men.

He preached deliverance to captives. They are not only captives who are in Long Bay or some other goal. Many have been held captive by moral weakness, evil thoughts, unholy desires, and having heard the preaching of Christ, been delivered from the chains of evil and experienced the freedom to serve Him even behind bars. He came to preach deliverance and make better men.

Recovering of sight to the blind. How can people be their best with such a handicap. Blindness is a sad affliction and great hinderance. Spiritual blindness is what God is concerned about. So many can't see God at work in the world, in nature, in man, in anything. Many can't see Him as a personal power in their life. He is kept for Churches and ministers. Things of this world have blinded them. They can't see over the mountains they have created around them. There was "No room in the inn"[3]. Would the Inn keeper have found room if he could have perceived the great event about to take place. Reverend Vernon says: - "He came to give sight to spiritually blinded eyes. That we may see the day of visitation, might perceive opportunity at our door, and recognize the glory of God in the face of Jesus Christ." When our eyes have been opened to see the Christ, we then are better, far better people.

He was sent to set at liberty them that are bruised. We can be bruised without being bound, hurt by the wrongdoing of others.

We go back to prophet Isaiah. "But he was wounded for our transgressions, he was bruised for our iniquities: the chastisement of our peace was upon him; and with his stripes we are healed."[4]

Ony when we come to Jesus and allow Him control of our lives, are we healed and become better men.

---

[1] Luke 4:18
[2] Luke 4:16-22
[3] Luke 2:7
[4] Isaiah 53:5

Mother's Day

One day of the year is set aside to pay public honour to our mothers. This one day means less than nothing if the other 364 days are not lived in the spirit of this day. Unless our mother is honoured, helped, and gladdened every day by our love and thoughtfulness, just to give a gift on Mother's Day is a mockery and hurts more than could be expressed. She would far rather us forget the gift and give our love. We can't really love her one day and ignore her all the rest.

A mother knows how her child feels toward her before she receives anything from them and knows exactly whether the gift is a token or an expression of sincere love. Quite apart from the gift, it is also about how it is given. Is it given to someone else to pass on? Just handed over, or given with great show of affection. It will be meaningless if the child does something to prove it was all just for the occasion and not deep or lasting. Real love has its own way of conveying its message and will always be seen in what it does more than what it says.

Honour father and mother, honour to whom honour is due. He that loveth father or mother more than me is not worthy of me. Are we pausing to give honour to our mothers today and bringing dishonour upon the one who gave us mothers, who placed within their hearts what we know as mothers' love. Mother has every right to expect us to love her, honour, and obey.

God's Day

Same applies to God's Day. This is not once a year but universally recognized as once a week. Remember the Sabbath Day.[1]

Many go to Church and take active part but there is very little love or honour to God. Some might even listen to the sermon, but all the time, feel resentful because something said is cutting across selfish ideas. If we really honoured God on this day we wouldn't think of anyone else's bad points, we'd forget ourselves and just long to show our love to Him, long to be near and hear His voice. Here too, every day must be God's Day.

---

[1] Exodus 20:8

Our Bodies – God's Temple

"Do you not know that your bodies are temples of the Holy Spirit, who is in you, whom you have received from God? You are not your own; you were bought at a price. Therefore, honour God with your bodies."[1]

Purity of the body, especially in connection with fornication drives home this very important truth which we should never forget but let sink deep, thrill our hearts, and encourage us and challenge us. We'll think of these two verses in five headings.

1 God's Temple. Stephen tells the Sanhedrin that the most high dwelleth not in temples made with hands.[2] Isaiah records for us God's declaration "for thus saith the high and lofty one that inhabetheth eternity whose names is Holy; I dwell in the high and holy place, with him also that is of a contrite and humble spirit."[3] Our bodies, we are the temples of God. God's dwelling place. "Don't you know that you yourselves are God's temple and that God's Spirit dwells in your midst? If anyone destroys God's temple, God will destroy that person; for God's temple is sacred, and you together are that temple."[4]

2 Defile. "Out of the heart", said Jesus, "proceed evil thoughts, murders, adulteries, fornication, thefts, false witness, blasphemies, these are the things which defile a man."[5] In Mark there are more added, covetousness, wickedness, deceit, lasciviousness (I.e. Lust) an evil eye, pride, foolishness.[6] James tells us "the tongue is a fire, a world of iniquity, it defileth the whole body. An unruly evil full of deadly poison, therewith bless we God and therewith curse we men which are made after the similitude of God".[7]

We are created to be God's temple, God's dwelling place, of worship, prayer, and fellowship with Him. When God comes, does He find it defiled. Whatever in our natures and our lives that is not of love defiles us and if we defile God's dwelling place, God will destroy us.

3 God's Ownership. Have we any right to take possession of a temple created by God for Himself. "Don't you know that you yourselves are God's temple and that God's Spirit dwells in your midst? If anyone destroys God's temple, God will destroy that person; for God's temple is sacred, and you together are that temple."[8] You are not your own is one of the last lessons we learn although the first God wants to teach us. "I'll please myself," "I'll be my own boss," "No one will tell me what to do," "I've got my own rights," are phrases which should never be heard in a Christians conversation. We are not our own. We are God's and God has the sole right to do what He wants with His own.

We stop here and ask ourselves, do we have too much say in what we'll do with our lives, time, talents, and possessions? When we are not our own, we haven't got a say.

4 God's Purchase. Ye are bought with a price. Peter tells us we "were not redeemed with corruptible things, *as* silver and gold, from your vain conversation *receive* by tradition from your fathers;"[9]. If someone paid over £100 to get us, we'd say they wanted us a good deal, think of this in the light of God Himself-giving himself. There was no other good enough to pay the price of sin, He only was good enough.

5 God's Purpose for Us. To glorify Him in our bodies and spirits. Every part must show that God has done great things. Every part must show God's hand. It's our great privilege to be able to reveal the work of God in a human life.

---

[1] 1 Cor 6:19-20
[2] Acts 7:48
[3] Isaiah 57:15
[4] 1 Cor 3:16-17
[5] Matthew 15:19
[6] Mark 7:22
[7] James 3:6-12
[8] 1 Corinthians 3:16-17
[9] 1 Peter 1:18

Our modern civilization

Our modern civilization offers us so many benefits most of which we take for granted. Take for example, the benefits of electricity. The ins and outs of its working is beyond our understanding, but the fact that it does work has been proved every day beyond any doubt. We know we can press a switch and receive power for quite a number of appliances. Think of the electrical equipment in your home or place of work.

Light: Could you work without light? Darkness means danger. Light is an absolute essential. Can we wonder, then, that Jesus said that He was the light of the world. In cold hard facts it means that if He is rejected, there is absolutely no light, therefore spiritual disaster results.

Our Cleaning Appliances: Washing machines, scrubbers, vacuum cleaners, dishwashers etc. Cleanliness is next to Godliness, or so we are told. How much harm is done simply because this is neglected. It is rather tragic to find people who are very particular about cleanliness in their work and person, forgetting that cleanliness must be used in our conversation, habits, desires, thoughts, and souls. Appliances have their place on the material level, but only Christ can clean those more important parts of our lives. He said on one occasion, "Now ye are clean through the word which I have spoken unto you"[1], Paul says, "If we confess our sins, he is faithful and just to forgive us our sins, and to cleanse us from all unrighteousness."[2]

We must have light, cleanliness, and we must have food and drink. Here a refrigerator, stove, mixer, jugs, and the like do their job. Good food must be preserved, and prepared well to do its best work and we are not fit for our best work without it. A very common mistake of life is to overfeed the body and starve the soul, or the feed it on rubbish. Bad reading matter, shady stories, trifling programmes, so much matter for the mind but so little provides nourishment for mind and heart.

Jesus again sets the standard, He said "I have meat to eat that ye know not of, my meat is to do the will of my father"[3] "Jesus saith unto them, My meat is to do the will of him that sent me, and to finish his work."[4] And what better advice can be given than the words of scripture. Desire the sincere milk of the word that you might grow thereby.[5]

So much more could be said regarding appliances and their particular role in life, but if we are unable to connect them to a power source, they are absolutely useless because, of themselves, they would only be ornaments. There is so much behind all this to make them work. If we trace it back, there is a tremendous network of wires, thousands of poles, a large staff of workers, and great cost even before we get to the source of supply, the powerhouse, but what a great concern this is. The round the clock activity in order that we might plug in day or night and receive power. Does this speak to your inner self and bring a spiritual truth? Do you realize that God Himself is our Spiritual powerhouse. "Jesus said, "All power is given unto me in Heaven and in earth"[6] Also, "ye shall receive power after that the Holy Spirit is come upon you"[7] So the Triune God has the power for the whole universe, and supplied it to us as individuals, not without tremendous cost to Himself. And without him we are useless. There is never a stoppage or breakdown, but the link is often broken. That link or connection is on our part. We must believe and obey. Electricity does not benefit those who don't believe in it or those who don't obey the simple rules.

Is your life useful, a blessing to those you meet because you are linked on to God and His power is coming through or is there a faulty connection? You don't really believe that God can and are not prepared to obey the urges toward the highest and best.

A powerless life is a denial of God but from now you can link on by receiving Christ in faith as your saviour from sin and obeying His word. For "To as many as received him, to them gave them power to become the sons of God even to them that believe on his name."[8]

Let the words of this hymn be your prayer as it is sung for us "I need thee every hour".[9]

---

[1] John 15:3
[2] 1 John 1:9
[3] John 4:32
[4] John 4:34
[5] 1 Peter 2:2
[6] Matthew 28:18
[7] Acts 1:8
[8] John 1:12
[9] 9 Annie S Hawks (verses) and Robert Lowry, "I need Thee every hour", The Song Book of The Salvation Army, (London, UK: SP&S), 606.

Prophecy against the House of Eli. 1 Sam 2:27-30

Few would say that they despise God. Yet, actions speak louder than words and men's lives declare more plainly than their lips, the fact that they have no time for God, and their real attitude to Him.

God speaks to us. We do not answer. If a neighbour speaks and we do not turn our head or answer him, wouldn't he be quite in order to say we rejected him.

God speaks through our conscience. We know what is right and wrong. We deliberately refuse God's speaking and choose the selfish disobedient choice.

God speaks through His word, and we can't find time to read it, things that bring a little pleasure to our own feelings are more important.

God speaks through the Holy Spirit. Prompting, directing, holding us back. Paul had an experience of this while he was travelling through Asia.[1] We can despise and grieve God by not seeking the full co-operation of His Spirit, refusing to do as He directs.

God speaks through His Servants. Sometimes we don't like God's voice speaking through other people. Someone's example rebukes our self-indulgence and self-satisfaction. God speaks, telling us that our lives should be just as fully consecrated.

Sometimes, someone may say something directly to us, in a meeting,[2] or in our hearing, and if it cuts across our own way of thinking and shows that we have failed and come short, it is hard to take.

To turn a deaf ear to any or all of these revelations of God, is to despise or reject Him.

What if we do not hear Him? The voices of the world are too loud. We are listening to them instead of God.

How do we treat God's commands?
He commands us to repent.
He commands us to be holy.
He commands us to serve Him wholeheartedly.
If we do not obey, then we are not honouring Him.

God's invitation. If we were invited to a friend's home but we did not go or even send an apology or reason, he could say we rejected his invitation. God's invitation is always extended to us to come unto Him.

God's gift of salvation. If we have refused to accept it, we are despising His offer if we do not yield to His will or obey His commands.

---

[1] Acts 16:6-7
[2] Meetings are a Salvation Army term for Church service which were more led by the Holy Spirit than following a ritual.

Right or Wrong

If a man put a news board upside down, we would ask why? Was it because he can't see, or he doesn't know which way it goes? Was he in too big a hurry? Probably not!

Maybe it was because he didn't take the trouble to check and see that its up the right way round.

He wouldn't even know that it was upside down unless he went back and checked it, or someone told him.

Many times in life there are two ways of doing things, a right and a wrong way, and this man did it wrong because of the lack of attention. If only he had taken just that bit of care to see that what he'd done was right.

God tells us in His word that there is a right way for us to reach Heaven. "Jesus saith unto him, ***I am the way, the truth***, **and the life:** no man cometh unto the Father, but by me."[1] This means that we need to make Jesus Lord of our lives, and if we don't, we will find that we will be unable to enter Heaven at the end of our time here on Earth.

It is also about making good choices in life. There is a right and wrong way to live our lives. "Whatsoever thy hand findeth to do, do *it* with thy might."[2] Some people live their lives upside down, by being careless about their health, relationships, and work. God wants us to live in a way that will honour Him. Reading His word, the Bible, is a good way for us to constantly check if our lives are up the right way or upside down. "All scripture *is* given by inspiration of God, and *is* profitable for doctrine, for reproof, for correction, for instruction in righteousness."[3]

---

[1] John 14:6
[2] Ecclesiastes 9:10
[3] 2 Timothy 3:16

The Story of Joseph

The story of Joseph is one of the favourite Old Testament stories especially with children. If you want an enjoyable hour with your Bible, read his story from where his father showed him favouritism right through to the end of his life[1]. It is full of interest and colour. It will grip your imagination as well as warm your heart. There is so much about him which we can take as a worthy example.

1 He knew God. We read that "God was with him". Here is the whole secret of his greatness. He was only great because He had a great God who worked out a great purpose in his life. He was living out the verse "but the people who do know their God shall be strong, and do exploits."[2]

2 He was dependable. How we like to have dealings with people who are reliable. Whether working in the garden or cleaning gutters or deciding matters of national importance – reliability is a characteristic we could well determine to cultivate. This means that the jobs done where no other person sees are done as thoroughly as those in full view and commendation of others. Joseph's faithfulness in small things paved the way to greater responsibilities.

3 He was a man of principle. He had plenty of occasion to lower his standards. He was tempted and force was even brought to bear upon him, but his standard was God's standard, and he refused to lower it. We have no more reason today to lower our standards and disregard principle than Joseph had. However, we so often do from fear of what others think, from fear of losing our position, but Joseph paid exactly this price for his standing up and doing what was right, and yet God honoured him through it all. Joseph had a real test to his faith and his patience through the neglect of one whom he had helped – remaining in prison for a further two years but he patiently waited for God's time, and by his devotion to duty and his faithfulness, he was ready when God's time came. There is so much more we could say about Joseph, but we can only leave you to read it for yourself from the book of Genesis. You will receive such a blessing and inspiration.

---

[1] Genesis 37-50
[2] Daniel 11:32

Author's Note.

This message was found in Mum's things, and was actually written by my grandmother, Elvie May Morris.

My Friend - Mrs Griffey.

In a homely room she lies, this friend of mine. For nearly nineteen years no other visitors have met her eyes but these four walls, except when she has had to spend time in hospital.

One day I asked her when she had first learned to know God and she replied, 'at my mother's knee when she taught us to pray'.

I knew something of the story of that mother, her mother was a nurse maid to a Christian lady on one of the stations which was in the back blocks of Australia in those early days of the pioneers. Where did you first Learn to know God? At my mother's knee when she taught us to pray. Happy is the mother whose child can make such an answer. Once again, I realized the importance of teaching the little ones to pray. How many people have entered the room of this lovely lady and had their minds turned toward God. How many times have I poured out a tale of sorrow to her and been comforted by her sympathy. Her story led me to write this poem called:

Teach them to pray.

They came to the country of promise rare
And bought with them a nursemaid fair
To a property in a lovely spot
Where they settled down to their happy lot

The lady of the household sought
To teach the nursemaid she had brought
To know her God and serve him too
For she knew that he would see her through

A Shepherd who was in the employ
Sought and won her to his joy
In a little cottage by the hill
She faced a life of good and ill
With a courage that did not fade away
And she taught her children how to pray
Were they hours that passed grave or gay

One at least has lived to tell
How the lessons learned, have stood her well
For though she now is laid aside
She tells, how the Lord, still does abide

In that room as you linger there
You lay aside a load of care
For who would at life fume and fret

When you see the sweetness that lingers yet
When you know the pain she daily bears
And how she for the souls of others cares
When she smiles a thank you for your love
She turns your mind to God above

For to Him she turns in the sleepless hour
In him alone she has strength and power
To many a one has new strength been given
By the prayers, that pour from her heart to Heaven
Thank you, God, we softly say,
For the mother who taught her how to pray

This mother died when her children were young in years, but the prayers taught by her are still remembered. After her death, the lady who had brought her out from England had the children come every Sunday to her home to teach them the word of God, that was between sixty and seventy years ago and the seed sown is still bearing fruit.

Just by way of interest this lady's descendants still live on the same station.

Other Books by this Author

<u>Devotionals</u>

Turning Water into Wine

More Water into Wine

Still More Water into Wine

365 Glasses of Wine

Conversations with Myself (volumes 1 and 2)

Reflections

Fireside Stories (with Wendy Brown)

<u>Fiction</u>

Christmas Journeys

Like Father, Like Son

You're: Healing Broken Hearts in Huntersville

<u>Poetry/Variety</u>

Whispers from on High

With the exception of 'Whispers From on High', all books are available in print and eBook formats

www.ingramcontent.com/pod-product-compliance
Lightning Source LLC
Chambersburg PA
CBHW041144110526
44590CB00027B/4117